OHIO TRIVIA

TRIVIA

REVISED EDITION

OHIO TRIVIA

COMPILED BY ERNIE & JILL COUCH

REVISED EDITION

Rutledge Hill Press
Nashville, Tennessee

Published by Rutledge Hill Press, Inc.,
211 Seventh Avenue North,
Nashville, Tennessee 37219

*Typography by ProtoType Graphics, Inc.
and D&T/Bailey Typography, Inc.*

Couch, Ernie, 1949-
  Ohio trivia/compiled by Ernie & Jill Couch.
    p.   cm.
  ISBN 1-55853-207-2
    1. Ohio—Miscellanea.   2. Questions and answers.
  I. Couch, Jill, 1948-   II. Title.
  F491.5.C68   1988   88-4979
  977.14'0076—dc19   CIP

Printed in the United States of America
2 3 4 5 6 7 8—95 94

PREFACE

When *Ohio Trivia* was originally compiled, it became evident that many volumes could be written about this fascinating state. Ohio is comprised of a richly diversified land and people with colorful traditions and a compelling history. Now the revised edition of *Ohio Trivia* captures even more interesting facts about this exciting heritage.

Ohio Trivia is designed to be informative, educational, and entertaining. But most of all we hope that you will be motivated to learn more about the great state of Ohio.

—Ernie & Jill Couch

To
Bob & Theresa Lischke
and
the great people of Ohio

TABLE OF CONTENTS

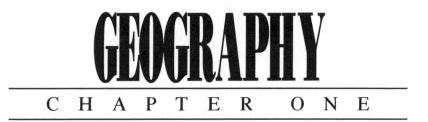

GEOGRAPHY

C H A P T E R   O N E

Q. What is the total distance between Ohio's northern and southern borders?

A. 210 miles.

Q. Where was the first Quaker meeting house west of the Alleghenies constructed in 1814?

A. Mount Pleasant.

Q. What is the meaning of the Indian word after which Geauga County is named?

A. "Raccoon."

Q. During the last half of the nineteenth century, what Ohio city was said to be the world's largest freshwater fish market?

A. Sandusky.

Q. How many covered bridges are there in Ohio?

A. 175.

Q. What Ohio town was formed in 1854 by a union of an early Quaker settlement and the communities of Freedom, Mount Union, and Williamsport?

A. Alliance.

Q. What is the northernmost reservoir shared by Ohio and Pennsylvania?

A. Pymatuning Reservoir.

Q. The summer home of Rutherford B. Hayes was on what Ohio island?

A. Mouse Island.

Q. What is the meaning of the Indian word after which Auglaize County is named?

A. "Fallen timbers."

Q. What Lorain County community was previously called Podunk and for a time nicknamed the "Little Whighole"?

A. South Amherst.

Q. Chillicothe is the seat of what county?

A. Ross.

Q. Ohio's oldest church building still in use is in what community?

A. Talmadge.

Q. What Ohio county is named for the Ottawa Indian word meaning "mother"?

A. Miami.

Q. What is the southernmost county in Ohio?

A. Lawrence.

Q. By what former name was the Hocking River called?

A. Hock-hocking or Bottle River.

Q. Nationally, where does Ohio rank in the number of miles of railroad track per square mile?

A. First.

Q. What body of water forms a large portion of Ohio's northern boundary?

A. Lake Erie.

Q. In what Ohio community was Ulysses S. Grant born?

A. Point Pleasant.

Q. In what Ohio town is the largest bascule-type lift bridge in the United States?

A. Lorain.

Q. What mining community with a Chinese name sprang into existence on the eastern edge of Perry County in 1900?

A. Santoy.

Q. What Ohio county is named after the Revolutionary War hero who captured Fort Ticonderoga in northeastern New York?

A. Allen (for Ethan Allen).

Q. Wright-Patterson Air Force Base is near what city?

A. Fairborn.

Q. On October 17, 1790, what Ohio settlement was founded by approximately five hundred French artisans and craftsmen?

A. Gallipolis.

Q. The world headquarters of Battelle Memorial Institute is in what Ohio city?

A. Columbus.

Q. Which city claims the title "Rubber Capital of the World"?

A. Akron.

Q. Toledo is on what bay?

A. Maumee.

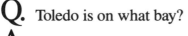

Q. After viewing a sunrise over what hills did William Creighton suggest the motif for the Ohio State seal?

A. Mount Logan Range.

———◆———

Q. What name is given to the portion of Meigs County that is surrounded on three sides by the Ohio River?

A. "The boot."

———◆———

Q. By what name was Ashland called when first platted in 1815?

A. Uniontown.

———◆———

Q. What northeast Allen County town founded in 1833 took its present name from an Indiana Mennonite community?

A. Bluffton.

———◆———

Q. In 1798 Michael Garver homesteaded land that evolved into what present-day community?

A. Troy.

———◆———

Q. The Pontifical College Josephinum is in what community?

A. Worthington.

———◆———

Q. Zanesville was established at the confluence of what two rivers?

A. Licking and Muskingum rivers.

Q. What Ohio city is home to Fort Meigs, the largest reconstructed fort in the nation?

A. Toledo.

Q. Georgetown is the seat of what county?

A. Brown.

Q. Who founded Lodi in 1824?

A. Judge Joseph Harris.

Q. World famous seismologist Charles F. Richter, developer of the Richter Scale, was born in what Ohio town in 1900?

A. Hamilton.

Q. In honor of what twins was Twinsburg named?

A. Moses and Aaron Wilcox.

Q. What community served as the seat of Meigs County from 1822 to 1841?

A. Chester.

Q. What Ohio county was named for the salt licks within its borders?

A. Licking.

Q. In 1867 William McKinley set up his law practice in what Ohio community?

A. Canton.

Q. How many counties did Ohio have at the time it became a state?

A. Nine.

Q. What museum and gift shop is the home of the "World's Largest Cuckoo Clock"?

A. Alpine-Alpa (in Wilmont).

Q. For whom is Lake Erie named?

A. An Indian tribe.

Q. Dayton produces more of what kind of business machines than any other city in the United States?

A. Cash registers.

Q. The Miami River Valley flood control project was finished in what year?

A. 1922.

Q. What county is named for the general who defeated the British at Lundy's Lane?

A. Brown (for Major General Jacob Brown).

Q. Whose statement, "I defy the English, the Indians, and all the devils in hell to take it," led to the naming of Defiance?

A. General Anthony ("Mad Anthony") Wayne.

Q. What is the longest tributary of the Ohio River in the state?

A. The Scioto River (237 miles).

Q. James A. Garfield, the last United States president born in a log cabin, was a native of what Ohio community?

A. Orange in Cuyahoga County.

Q. An Arabian city is the source of what Ohio county's name?

A. Medina.

Q. In honor of what Connecticut governor was an Ohio county named in 1800?

A. Jonathan Trumbull.

Q. What 1807 structure is the oldest house in Warren?

A. John Stark Edwards House.

Q. In what city is Walsh College?

A. Canton.

Q. What Ohio city is the "home of the steam shovel"?

A. Marion.

Q. How wide is Kelleys Island at its widest point?

A. Seven miles.

Q. For what reason was Richland County given its name on March 1, 1808?

A. The rich, fertile soil in the area.

Q. What school for chorister training was established in 1926 at Dayton?

A. The Westminster Choir School.

Q. What Ashtabula house became famous as a station on the Underground Railroad?

A. The Hubbard Homestead.

Q. From where in 1789 did John Cleve Symmes bring settlers to found Cincinnati?

A. New Jersey.

Q. Bay Bridge was established in 1892 as a company town built around what industry?

A. Cement manufacturing.

Q. What Greene County community is named for an English reformer who opposed slave trade?

A. Wilberforce (for William Wilberforce).

Q. In the early 1830s what community became a popular ferrying point across the Ohio River for large numbers of hogs, sheep, and cattle for eastern markets?

A. Martins Ferry.

Q. What title has been given to East Liverpool?

A. "Pottery Center of America."

Q. What is the meaning of the Indian word after which Mahoning County is named?

A. "At the licks."

Q. Built between 1869 and 1880, what was the first and only municipally owned steam railroad in the world?

A. Southern Railway (in Cincinnati).

Q. Shipwrecked Chicago-bound Scottish immigrants founded what Lake Erie community?

A. Port Clinton.

Q. What community founded for mining operations is on the Marblehead peninsula between Lake Erie and Sandusky Bay?

A. Gypsum.

Q. The annual return of buzzards prompted Hinckley to name March 15 what day?

A. Buzzard Day.

Q. What Lake Erie coastal community has been called the "Plymouth" of the Western Reserve?

A. Conneaut.

Q. What is the meaning of the Indian word after which Muskingum is named?

A. "By the river side."

Q. To what Ohio community did Joseph Smith, founder of the Mormon religion, move his organization's headquarters in January of 1831?

A. Kirtland.

Q. Being at the highest elevation along the Ohio canal gave what county its name?

A. Summit.

Q. Patrick Good submitted the winning name drawn from a hat for what Ohio city?

A. Lima.

Q. What Logan County point is the highest elevation in Ohio?

A. Campbell Hill (1,550 feet above sea level).

Q. What large natural feature in the northwestern section of Ohio was a hindrance to early settlers?

A. The Black Swamp.

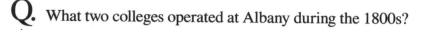

Q. What two colleges operated at Albany during the 1800s?

A. Atwood Institute and Enterprise Institute.

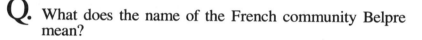

Q. John Studebaker, father of Henry and Clement Studebaker of automotive fame, built a house and blacksmith shop in what county in 1835?

A. Wayne.

———◆———

Q. What does the name of the French community Belpre mean?

A. "Beautiful meadows."

———◆———

Q. Overlooking Lancaster, Mount Pleasant was called by what name by the Indians?

A. Standing Stone.

———◆———

Q. Civil War General Philip Henry Sheridan spent his boyhood in what Perry County community?

A. Somerset.

———◆———

Q. What Crawford County community is named for a famous Seminole Indian chief?

A. Oceola.

Q. What Morgan County community is known for its "happy" name?

A. Joy.

Q. Where in 1788 was the first permanent settlement in the Northwest Territory established?

A. Marietta.

Q. What two major lakes are contained in Harrison County?

A. Clendening Lake and Tappan Lake.

Q. For whom did Colonel Thomas Poague name Fort Amanda, which he constructed on the Auglaize River in 1812?

A. His wife.

Q. Where was President Benjamin Harrison born in 1833?

A. North Bend.

Q. What is the meaning of the name *Gallipolis*, first given by its French founders in the late eighteenth century?

A. "City of Gauls."

Q. Approximately how many square miles make up the state of Ohio?

A. 41,000.

Q. Where did Union troops engage some 900 armed local residents during the Holmes County Rebellion of 1863?

A. "Fort Fizzle" (near Glenmont).

Q. For whom was the city of Dayton named?

A. Jonathan Dayton, youngest signer of the U.S. Constitution, who lived nearby.

Q. By what name was Kelleys Island known around 1800?

A. Cunningham's Island.

Q. What is the name of the twenty-six-room former home of James A. Garfield in Mentor?

A. Lawnfield.

Q. The last survivor of the signers of the Declaration of Independence is honored by what county name?

A. Carroll County (for Charles Carroll).

Q. What is the meaning of the Indian word *Erie?*

A. "Cat."

Q. What city in 1884 became the first in Ohio to offer an electric street railway system?

A. Cleveland.

Q. Bellefontaine was built on the site of what Shawnee village?

A. Blue Jacket's Town.

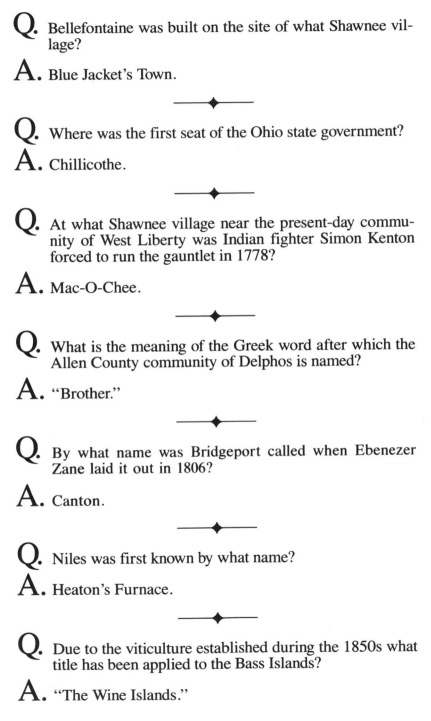

Q. Where was the first seat of the Ohio state government?

A. Chillicothe.

Q. At what Shawnee village near the present-day community of West Liberty was Indian fighter Simon Kenton forced to run the gauntlet in 1778?

A. Mac-O-Chee.

Q. What is the meaning of the Greek word after which the Allen County community of Delphos is named?

A. "Brother."

Q. By what name was Bridgeport called when Ebenezer Zane laid it out in 1806?

A. Canton.

Q. Niles was first known by what name?

A. Heaton's Furnace.

Q. Due to the viticulture established during the 1850s what title has been applied to the Bass Islands?

A. "The Wine Islands."

Q. What Ohio county was named for the current vice president of the United States when it was founded on March 1, 1810?

A. Clinton (for Vice President George Clinton).

Q. The pioneer communities of Rome and Risdon united under what name in 1854?

A. Fostoria.

Q. What creek flows into the Ohio River at Clarington?

A. Sunfish Creek.

Q. Where was General George Custer born on December 5, 1839?

A. New Rumley.

Q. Hole's Station, laid out in 1818 by Zachariah Hole, bears what present-day name?

A. Miamisburg.

Q. Jacob's Well, named for early pioneer Jacob Foos who dug a well there, changed to what name in 1822?

A. Marion.

Q. What community was established by German Separatists in 1817–18 in northern Tuscarawas County?

A. Zoar.

Q. Where does Ohio rank among the other states in the total value of manufactured goods?

A. Third.

Q. What Highland County community was the site of the Society of Friends' annual meeting prior to 1900?

A. Leesburg.

Q. What 1836 Maumee stagecoach stop and present-day restaurant was host to Presidents Lincoln, Garfield, and Harding?

A. J. R. Brown's River Inn.

Q. The Delaware Indian word meaning "union of waters" is the name of what Ohio county?

A. Coshoctan.

Q. What religious structure of unique architecture and modern technology may be seen in Cuyahoga Falls?

A. The Cathedral of Tomorrow.

Q. What community led Ohio in the shipping of coal via the Ohio River prior to 1850?

A. Pomeroy.

Q. What Ohio island served as a prisoner of war camp during the Civil War?

A. Johnson's Island.

Q. Ohio is known by what nickname?

A. The Buckeye State.

Q. What are the four major land regions of Ohio?

A. Great Lakes Plains, the Till Plains, the Appalachian Plateau, and the Bluegrass Region.

Q. What reservoir was completed in 1915 as a water supply for Akron?

A. Lake Rockwell.

Q. Where was President Warren G. Harding born in 1865?

A. Near Corsica.

Q. A Virginia Baptist minister created what Lawrence County community by providing land for his freed slaves?

A. Burlington.

Q. The Fisher brothers, noted for the manufacture of automobile bodies, spent their early years in what Huron County community?

A. Norwalk.

Q. The name of the Tuscarawas County community of Gnadenhutten has what meaning?

A. "Tents of grace."

Q. Warring factions of ruffians burned what Montgomery County community in 1876?

A. New Lebanon.

Q. What Henry County community shares its name with a state?

A. Texas.

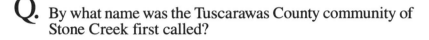

Q. By what name was the Tuscarawas County community of Stone Creek first called?

A. Phillipsburg (for Phillip Leonard).

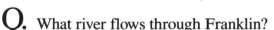

Q. What river flows through Franklin?

A. The Great Miami.

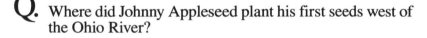

Q. Where did Johnny Appleseed plant his first seeds west of the Ohio River?

A. On Licking Creek (near Etna).

Q. An English poet is honored in the name of what Shelby County community?

A. Sidney (for Sir Philip Sidney).

Q. How many stories tall is the Terminal Tower in Cleveland?

A. Fifty-two.

Q. Pickaway County derives its name from a variant of what Indian word?

A. *Piqua.*

Q. Because of the early concentration of Quakers, what community became known as "Ohio's City of Friends"?

A. Salem.

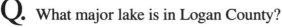

Q. What major lake is in Logan County?

A. Indian Lake.

Q. Where was the first Episcopal church in Ohio organized in 1803?

A. Worthington.

Q. During the mid-1800s what inland Erie County community became one of the world's largest and busiest grain shipping centers?

A. Milan.

Q. Where does Ohio rank in area among all the states?

A. Thirty-fifth.

Q. What county received its name because it bordered Lake Erie?

A. Lake.

Q. In 1898 Missouri businessman Henry H. Timken selected what Ohio city for the manufacture of his newly patented roller bearing?

A. Canton.

———◆———

Q. From what source does Athens County derive its name?

A. The capital city of Greece.

———◆———

Q. Maumee is a corruption of what Indian name?

A. *Miami*.

———◆———

Q. The Wright Brothers Memorial is in what Ohio city?

A. Dayton.

———◆———

Q. When laid out in 1814, Cuba in Clinton County was given what name?

A. Paris.

———◆———

Q. The creation of what county from portions of four other counties led to its descriptive name?

A. Union.

———◆———

Q. Where was the noted lawyer and agnostic Clarence Darrow born in 1857?

A. Farmdale (near Kinsman).

Q. Milan was founded on the site of the former Indian village of Pequotting whose name had what meaning?

A. "Pay nothing."

Q. Lima is on what river?
A. The Ottawa.

Q. A stagecoach wreck in 1836 on the National Road involving Henry Clay and a party of congressmen led to the naming of what depression near Mount Sterling?

A. Congress Hollow.

Q. What Ohio city has hosted three national political conventions?

A. Cincinnati (Democratic, 1856 and 1830; Republican, 1876).

Q. Until 1888 Norwood was called by what name?
A. Sharpsburg (for John Sharp).

Q. Where was American clergyman Norman Vincent Peale born in 1898?

A. Bowersville.

Q. What was the original name of Reading?
A. Vorheestown.

Q. How far is the distance between the eastern and western boundaries of Ohio?

A. 225 miles.

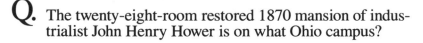

Q. The twenty-eight-room restored 1870 mansion of industrialist John Henry Hower is on what Ohio campus?

A. University of Akron.

Q. The governor's mansion is in what Columbus suburb?

A. Bexley.

Q. What present Ohio municipality evolved from the early communities of Croghansville and Lower Sandusky?

A. Fremont.

Q. What is the Ohio state motto?

A. With God All Things Are Possible.

Q. What major Cleveland suburb was known as East Rockport before 1889?

A. Lakewood.

Q. What states border Ohio?

A. Michigan, Pennsylvania, West Virginia, Kentucky, and Indiana.

Q. Where was Harvey Samuel Firestone born in 1868?

A. Columbiana.

Q. A Mingo Indian village was the site of what present-day Ashland County community?

A. Jeromesville.

Q. Where does Ohio rank among other states in the number of miles of surfaced highways?

A. Fifth.

Q. In what community did William McKinley plead his first law case?

A. Hayesville.

Q. Who was the first white man to settle in Van Wert County?

A. Captain James Watson Riley.

Q. The site of the Cleveland suburb of Bedford was first given what name by Moravian settlers in 1786?

A. Pilgerruh.

Q. What militant abolitionist spent part of his youth and adulthood at Hudson?

A. John Brown.

Q. Where was business magnet and political boss Marcus A. Hanna born in 1837?

A. Lisbon.

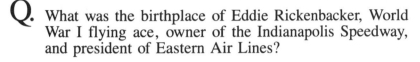

Q. What was the birthplace of Eddie Rickenbacker, World War I flying ace, owner of the Indianapolis Speedway, and president of Eastern Air Lines?

A. Columbus.

Q. How many electoral votes are allocated to Ohio?

A. Twenty-one.

Q. Which is the smallest land region in Ohio?

A. The Bluegrass Region.

Q. Incorporated in November of 1979, what Dayton suburb was officially proclaimed a city in January of 1980?

A. Beavercreek.

Q. What Ohio county is named for the secretary of war under George Washington?

A. Knox (for General Henry Knox).

Q. Ohio is comprised of how many counties?

A. Eighty-eight.

Q. Hollanders founded what southwest Huron County community in 1904?

A. Celeryville.

———◆———

Q. Where was the nation's first hospital for epileptics established in 1890?

A. Kanauga.

———◆———

Q. What was the first settlement in Summit County?

A. Hudson.

———◆———

Q. The North Branch, Middle Branch, South Branch, and East Branch combine to form what river in Ohio?

A. The Portage River.

———◆———

Q. Loudonville was named for what Revolutionary War soldier?

A. James Louden Priest.

———◆———

Q. Ashland and Pickaway counties contain communities with what name in common?

A. Five Points.

———◆———

Q. Whetstone and Youngstown were both former names of what Morrow County community?

A. Mount Gilead.

Q. On what island is the Perry's Victory and International Peace Memorial situated?

A. South Bass Island.

Q. By what name did the French call the Ohio River?

A. La Belle Rivière ("the beautiful river").

Q. Who laid out Toronto in Jefferson County under the name of Newburg in 1818?

A. John Dupuy.

Q. What is the largest municipality in Holmes County?

A. Millersburg.

Q. What Sandusky County community was originally called Cashtown because it had the first store in the county that paid cash for farm produce?

A. Hessville.

Q. How many acres are contained in Youngstown's Mill Creek Park?

A. Over 2,400.

Q. What does the bundle of seventeen arrows on the state seal represent?

A. Admission to the Union as the seventeenth state.

Q. Where does Ohio rank nationally in the number of cities having a population of over 500,000?

A. Second (California and Texas tie for first place).

———◆———

Q. What three Ohio communities whose names start with the letter *A* each contain only three letters in their name?

A. Ada, Aid, and Ava.

———◆———

Q. Plain City is on what creek?

A. Big Darby Creek.

———◆———

Q. What county is named in honor of the Revolutionary War officer who earned the nickname "Swamp Fox"?

A. Marion (for General Francis Marion).

———◆———

Q. What Ohio community is built on the site of the former Delaware Indian capital Gekelemukpechunk?

A. Newcomerstown.

———◆———

Q. Baldwin-Wallace College is in what Ohio town?

A. Berea.

———◆———

Q. "Cold water" is the meaning of what Indian place name?

A. Sandusky.

Q. In 1796 what name did surveyor Moses Cleaveland want to assign to the Ashtabula River?

A. Mary Esther (in honor of his daughter).

———◆———

Q. Ohio State University is on the banks of what river?

A. Olentangy River.

———◆———

Q. What is the meaning of the Indian word after which Tuscarawas County and Tuscarawas River are named?

A. "Open mouth."

———◆———

Q. In what locality is the Ohio Ceramic Center situated?

A. Crooksville.

———◆———

Q. What was the seat of Wood County from 1822 to 1866?

A. Perrysburg.

———◆———

Q. Joseph Gorden gave what Wood County community the name of his Kentucky hometown in 1835?

A. Bowling Green.

———◆———

Q. What is Ohio's leading manufacturing activity?

A. Transportation equipment.

Q. Where does Ohio rank in population compared to the other states?

A. Seventh.

———◆———

Q. What county and river are named with an Indian word that means "crooked"?

A. Cuyahoga.

———◆———

Q. What was the name of the estate that John D. Rockefeller established near Cleveland in 1876?

A. Forrest Hill.

———◆———

Q. The former estate of Rutherford B. Hayes is maintained in what state park?

A. Spiegel Grove State Park.

———◆———

Q. Both St. Clair and Fawcett's Town were early names applied to what present-day Ohio city?

A. Liverpool.

———◆———

Q. What crime caused the settlement of the town of Jackson in the early 1800s?

A. Boats belonging to a group of Welsh immigrants traveling down the Ohio River were stolen, so they remained there.

———◆———

Q. What is the largest single university campus in the nation?

A. Ohio State University at Columbus.

Q. Ohio's shoreline along Lake Erie extends for how many miles?

A. 312 (including Sandusky Bay and along the offshore islands).

———◆———

Q. What deep geological feature is a few miles east of Newark?

A. Black Hand Gorge.

———◆———

Q. Kansas is on the northern edge of what county?

A. Seneca.

———◆———

Q. Educator and college administrator William Rainey Harper was born in what Muskingum County community in 1856?

A. New Concord.

———◆———

Q. What Youngstown suburb was originally named Fowlers?

A. Poland.

———◆———

Q. What Ohio county received its name because of its level land?

A. Champaign County (from the French word meaning "a plain").

———◆———

Q. What is the largest metropolitan population area in the state?

A. Cleveland and vicinity.

Q. Cincinnati is known by what nickname?

A. "The Queen City."

Q. What Ohio county is named for a province in France?

A. Lorain (for the province of Lorraine).

Q. For whom was Chardon, the seat of Geauga County, named?

A. Peter Chardon Brooks.

Q. Situated only one and one-half miles south of the Canadian border, North Bass Island was first known by what name by the Postal Service?

A. The Isle of St. George.

Q. The seat of Perry County was moved to New Lexington from what community in 1857?

A. Somerset.

Q. What Cuyahoga County municipality is named for a Greek mathematician?

A. Euclid.

Q. In whose honor is Adams County named?

A. President John Quincy Adams.

Q. What fort stood near Kenton at one time?

A. Fort McArthur.

Q. General William Tecumseh Sherman was born in what Ohio municipality?

A. Lancaster.

Q. Where is Ohio Northern University?

A. Ada.

Q. A collection of 73,000 buttons, no two alike, may be seen in what city?

A. Dover, at Warther's.

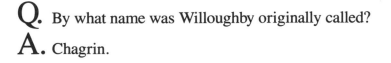

Q. Who founded Mount Sterling in 1828 and named it in honor of his former Kentucky home?

A. John J. Smith.

Q. By what name was Willoughby originally called?

A. Chagrin.

Q. Where was the first British fort in Ohio built in 1745?

A. Sandusky Bay (Fort Sandoski).

Q. When established in 1832, Winesburg was called by what name?

A. Weinsburgs.

───────◆───────

Q. Lorain sits at the mouth of what river?

A. Black.

───────◆───────

Q. The discovery of artesian wells led to the early development of what Williams County community?

A. Bryan.

───────◆───────

Q. What metropolis is known as the "Glass Capital of the World"?

A. Toledo.

───────◆───────

Q. What geographical feature divides the city of Cleveland?

A. The Cuyahoga River.

───────◆───────

Q. For whom is Pike County named?

A. General Zebulon M. Pike.

───────◆───────

Q. What large body of water is known as the "Walleye Capital of the World"?

A. Lake Erie.

Q. Legally, what two terms are used to designate all communities within Ohio?

A. Cities or villages.

Q. Who purchased Gibraltar Island for a summer house in 1864?

A. Financier Jay Cooke.

Q. Considered one of the finest examples of Tudor Revival architecture in the United States, Stan Hywet Hall at Akron was built by what industrialist?

A. Frank A. Seiberling.

Q. By what title were Connecticut's land holdings in Ohio territory called?

A. The Western Reserve.

Q. For whom was Mansfield named?

A. Jared Mansfield (surveyor general of the United States).

Q. Who named Johnsville?

A. John Ely.

Q. What Ohio city is the third largest port on the Great Lakes?

A. Toledo.

Q. Many gypsy kings and queens of the Pierce and Stanley tribes are buried in what Montgomery County cemetery?

A. Woodland Cemetery (near Dayton).

Q. What Ohio city is headquarters for the giant Kroger supermarket chain?

A. Cincinnati.

Q. Camp Perry, famous for its marksmanship competitions, is in what county?

A. Ottawa.

Q. The geographical center of Ohio is in what county?

A. Delaware.

Q. What Pike County creek was dammed in 1935 to create White Lake?

A. Pee Pee Creek.

Q. The Churches of God, General Conference, have headquarters in what Ohio community?

A. Findlay.

Q. What county's unusual octagonal courthouse was destroyed by fire in 1841?

A. Pickaway (at Circleville).

ENTERTAINMENT

C H A P T E R   T W O

Q. The international hit "Hang On Sloopy," composed by Celina-born guitarist Rick Derringer, was recorded by what Dayton band in 1965?

A. The McCoys.

Q. What Cincinnati-born actress starred with Rosemary Clooney, Bing Crosby, and Danny Kaye in the holiday film classic *White Christmas?*

A. Vera-Ellen.

Q. Dayton-born actor Gordon Jump played the character Arthur Carlson in what highly successful television sitcom?

A. "WKRP in Cincinnati."

Q. What famous gospel quartet has headquarters in Stow?

A. The Cathedral Quartet.

Q. Who is the star of the show at Sea World, southeast of Cleveland in Aurora?

A. Shamu, the Killer Whale.

Q. In what vacant Columbus high school was the 1984 movie *Teachers* filmed?

A. Central High School.

Q. What Cincinnati native was the tenor soloist for the Count Basie orchestra from 1953 to 1964?

A. Frank Benjamin Foster.

Q. The movie producer/director Steven Spielberg of *ET* fame is a native of what city?

A. Cincinnati.

Q. On what Cleveland radio station did deejay Alan Freed first spin the beginnings of rock'n'roll?

A. WJW.

Q. Life in a mid-1800s Ohio village can be enjoyed at what Archbold attraction?

A. Sauder Farm and Craft Village.

Q. What renowned Cleveland-born producer created such films as *Flower Drum Song, Thoroughly Modern Millie,* and *Airport?*

A. Ross Hunter.

Q. In what city did Phil Donahue first work as a television announcer?

A. Cleveland.

Q. Jim Backus became best known for his role in "Gilligan's Island" portraying what character?

A. Thurston Howell III.

———◆———

Q. What award-winning 1984 film about Willie, an immigrant from Hungary, was shot partially in Cleveland?

A. *Stranger Than Paradise*.

———◆———

Q. In 1967 Jim Fox formed what popular trio from members of other Cleveland bands?

A. The James Gang.

———◆———

Q. What actor was born Dino Crocetti in Steubenville on June 7, 1917?

A. Dean Martin.

———◆———

Q. Cincinnati-born Charles Fries produced what 1982 feline fantasy-horror film?

A. *Cat People*.

———◆———

Q. Where is Friar Tuck's Cabaret Theatre?

A. Maumee.

———◆———

Q. What Middletown native was a featured soloist with the Bob Crosby, Woody Herman, Artie Shaw, and Benny Goodman bands in the 1930s and 1940s?

A. Billy Batterfield.

Q. Cincinnati-born Roy Rogers broke into show business while singing for what group?

A. The Sons of the Pioneers.

———◆———

Q. What Lima-born actor received an Oscar in 1949 for his supporting role in *12 O'Clock High?*

A. Dean Jagger.

———◆———

Q. Actor Clark Gable worked at what occupation before launching his acting career?

A. A factory worker in an Akron rubber plant.

———◆———

Q. What Cleveland-born vocalist had a 1975 international hit with the ballad "All By Myself"?

A. Eric Carmen.

———◆———

Q. The nation's first moving picture peep show machine was patented by what Cincinnatian on February 5, 1861?

A. S. D. Goodale.

———◆———

Q. What Cincinnati-born actress has appeared in television's "Quincy," "Simon and Simon," and "Divorce Court"?

A. Teryn Patrice.

———◆———

Q. What Youngstown-born actor plays Al Bundy on the TV show "Married with Children"?

A. Ed O'Neill.

Q. What Cincinnati-born television soap star portrayed characters in "The Secret Storm," "Somerset," and "The Edge of Night"?

A. Joel Crothers.

Q. Singer/guitarist Tracy Chapman, best known for her recording "Fast Car," was born in what city?

A. Cleveland.

Q. What Akron native served as the first host of the TV game show "Concentration"?

A. Hugh Downs.

Q. What Cleveland-born actor portrayed Tom Willis on the TV comedy "The Jeffersons"?

A. Franklin Cover.

Q. Comic actor Tim Conway was born in what Ohio community?

A. Willoughby.

Q. What Ohio-born actress played Simka Gravas in the television comedy series "Taxi"?

A. Carol Kane.

Q. What Woodington-born commentator brought the far-away world into the lives of millions of Americans through radio, newsreels, and television?

A. Lowell Thomas.

Q. Where was country music singer Johnny Paycheck born?

A. Greenfield.

———————◆———————

Q. What Ohioan was co-host with Mel Torme of the musical series "Summertime U.S.A."?

A. Teresa Brewer.

———————◆———————

Q. As the villain Jack McCall in the 1936 Paramount western *The Plainsman,* what Cincinnati-born actor shot Gary Cooper in the back?

A. Clifford Porter Hall.

———————◆———————

Q. What outdoor entertainment center featuring rodeos, circus, and concerts is situated at Parkman?

A. Entertainment U.S.A.

———————◆———————

Q. At age four, comedian Bob Hope moved with his family to what Ohio city?

A. Cleveland.

———————◆———————

Q. What Cleveland-born actress played the role of Aunt Esther on TV's "Sanford and Son"?

A. LaWanda Page.

———————◆———————

Q. Toledo native John Blair, who has performed with such stars as Johnny Mathis, James Brown, and Stevie Wonder, plays what instrument?

A. Vitar.

Q. In what eastern Ohio community was actor Robert Urich born?

A. Toronto.

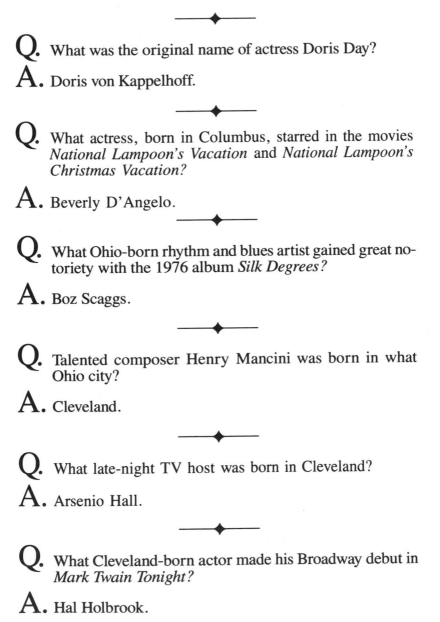

Q. What was the original name of actress Doris Day?

A. Doris von Kappelhoff.

Q. What actress, born in Columbus, starred in the movies *National Lampoon's Vacation* and *National Lampoon's Christmas Vacation?*

A. Beverly D'Angelo.

Q. What Ohio-born rhythm and blues artist gained great notoriety with the 1976 album *Silk Degrees?*

A. Boz Scaggs.

Q. Talented composer Henry Mancini was born in what Ohio city?

A. Cleveland.

Q. What late-night TV host was born in Cleveland?

A. Arsenio Hall.

Q. What Cleveland-born actor made his Broadway debut in *Mark Twain Tonight?*

A. Hal Holbrook.

Q. Phyllis Diller is a native of what Ohio city?

A. Lima.

———◆———

Q. What Dayton-born actor played station manager Andy Travis on "WKRP in Cincinnati"?

A. Gary Sandy.

———◆———

Q. Joel Grey, who was born in Cleveland, won an Oscar for best supporting actor in what 1972 film?

A. *Cabaret.*

———◆———

Q. What former Ms. Black Ohio co-hosted "NFL Today" on CBS?

A. Jayne Kennedy.

———◆———

Q. What successful talk show first aired on WLWD-TV, Dayton, on November 6, 1967?

A. "The Phil Donahue Show."

———◆———

Q. What Warren native was the regular drummer on "The Merv Griffin Show"?

A. Nick Ceroli.

———◆———

Q. Columbus, Galloway, and West Jefferson provided the scenery for what 1985 NBC Movie-of-the-Week starring Stephanie Zimbalist?

A. *Love on the Run.*

Q. What Cedarville-born actress played the baroness in the great movie musical *The Sound of Music*?

A. Eleanor Parker.

Q. Where was actor Gordon Jump born?

A. Dayton.

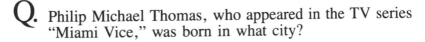

Q. Philip Michael Thomas, who appeared in the TV series "Miami Vice," was born in what city?

A. Columbus.

Q. What Cambridge-born writer created the ABC television series "The Guns of Will Sonnett"?

A. Richard Carr.

Q. Ohio native Catherine Bach played what character in the CBS hit series "The Dukes of Hazzard"?

A. Daisey Duke.

Q. Dayton-born actor Martin Sheen portrayed a reporter named Walker in what 1983 epic film?

A. *Gandhi*.

Q. What was the major Ohio location for the film *Mischief*?

A. Nelsonville.

Q. In what Ohio community was actor/comedian Paul Lynde born?

A. Mount Vernon.

Q. Henry Mancini received his first Oscar for what song?

A. "Moon River" (1962).

Q. In 1967 what Cleveland native and successful producer formed Lorimar Productions?

A. Lee Rich.

Q. Cincinnati-born actress Doris Day made her 1948 screen debut in what film?

A. *Romance on the High Seas*.

Q. Who was the first Ohio governor to lobby the film industry in Los Angeles for location filming?

A. Governor Richard F. Celeste.

Q. What 1979 film made in Cleveland starred Paul Simon?

A. *One Trick Pony*.

Q. Guitarist Ric Ocasek of Cleveland formed what successful rock'n'roll group in 1976?

A. The Cars.

Q. Michael J. Fox co-starred with Joan Jett in what 1986 contemporary drama filmed in Cleveland?

A. *Light of Day.*

---◆---

Q. What director/choreographer was born in Ashtabula?

A. Richard Barstow.

---◆---

Q. Toledo native Jamie Farr played what lovable crazy character on TV's "M*A*S*H"?

A. Corporal Max Klinger.

---◆---

Q. Cannonball Adderly discovered what Chillicothe-born singer who became a major star in the 1960s?

A. Nancy Wilson.

---◆---

Q. What city was host for the making of the television mini-series "The Jesse Owens Story"?

A. Columbus.

---◆---

Q. Columbus-born Tom Poston was what lovable character on TV's "Newhart" series?

A. George Utley (the handyman).

---◆---

Q. Cleveland provided the setting for what 1965 movie starring Jack Lemmon?

A. *Fortune Cookie.*

Q. What Columbus native portrayed Eleanor Roosevelt in the 1979 miniseries "Backstairs at the White House"?

A. Eileen Heckart.

Q. Where was writer/TV personality Erma Bombeck born?

A. Dayton.

Q. What Cleveland-born writer/director is credited with the television series "Dr. Kildare," "Lobo," and "Simon & Simon"?

A. Corey Allen.

Q. Where was the nation's first recorded Baby Show held on October 5, 1854?

A. Springfield.

Q. What Dayton-born trumpeter was a member of the "Tonight Show" band from 1962 to 1972?

A. Eugene ("Snooky") Young.

Q. Paul Newman is a native of what Ohio city?

A. Cleveland.

Q. In 1950 what recording became the biggest pop hit for Toledo native Teresa Brewer?

A. "Music, Music, Music."

Q. Known for composing jingles and TV spots, what Dayton native also did solos in the movies *Sandpiper, Charly,* and *The Summer of '42?*

A. Clifford E. ("Bud") Shank, Jr.

Q. Henry Mancini, famous composer of "Moon River," "Days of Wine & Roses," and the "Pink Panther Theme," was born in what Ohio city?

A. Cleveland.

Q. Ashtabula native Don Novello created what comic character seen on "Saturday Night Live"?

A. Father Guido Sarducci.

Q. Prison reform was the subject of what 1980 movie filmed in Perry, Fairfield, and Ross counties?

A. *Brubaker.*

Q. What was the original name of the Cleveland-born actor Joel Grey?

A. Joe Katz.

Q. Columbus-born Harry Edison, a trumpet player in the Count Basie band (1937–50), was called by what nickname?

A. Sweets.

Q. Cincinnati hosted the shooting of what 1980 CBS film starring Brenda Vacarro and Johnny Cash?

A. *The Pride of Jesse Hallam.*

Q. What Cincinnati-born actress appeared in such films as *Invitation to a Gunfighter, The Chase,* and *Missing?*

A. Janice Rule.

Q. Paul Lynde played what character on the long-running situation comedy "Bewitched"?

A. Uncle Arthur.

Q. Piqua is the birthplace of what famous family singing act?

A. The Mills Brothers.

Q. *Centennial,* a 1978 television movie, was filmed in Amish country at what restored 1830s canal town?

A. Roscoe Village.

Q. What television talk show personality was born in Canton?

A. Jack Paar.

Q. Clem Bevans, a character actor of the 1930s, 1940s, and 1950s, was born in what Ohio community on October 16, 1879?

A. Cozaddale.

Q. Robert Urich starred as what character in the successful crime show "VEGA$"?

A. Dan Tanna.

Q. What Dayton-born improvisationist began his show business career as a deejay in Dayton and Columbus?

A. Jonathan Winters.

------◆------

Q. Warren-born producer/director Roger Ailes became executive producer of what 1981 NBC late-night talk show?

A. "Tomorrow Coast to Coast."

------◆------

Q. What Steubenville firm is noted for its creation of animated figures and costumed characters?

A. Creegan Company.

------◆------

Q. Clark Gable was born in what Harrison County community?

A. Cadiz.

------◆------

Q. Ohioan Hal Holbrook starred as Father Malone in what 1980 thriller motion picture?

A. *The Fog.*

------◆------

Q. What rock group formed in 1957 actually began by singing gospel in their hometown of Cincinnati?

A. The Isley Brothers.

------◆------

Q. Austinburg, Conneaut, and Mentor provided the locations for what 1977 NBC movie starring Bette Davis and Joanna Miles?

A. *Harvest Home.*

Q. What Toledo-born actor was the voice for such famous cartoon characters as Yogi Bear, Huckleberry Hound, and Peter Potamus?

A. Daws Butler.

———◆———

Q. Where was singer/actress Kaye Ballard born?

A. Cleveland.

———◆———

Q. What Rocky River-born band leader composed the songs "Hawaiian Sunset" and "Wanderin'"?

A. Sammy Kaye.

———◆———

Q. Youngstown native Elizabeth Hartman was the voice of Mrs. Brisby in what 1982 feature-length Disney cartoon?

A. *The Secret of NIMH.*

———◆———

Q. What famous Ohio writer has written over 200 television scripts for NBC's "Wild Kingdom"?

A. Allan W. Eckert.

———◆———

Q. What "earresistible" celebration featuring square dancing, bluegrass music, and hot buttered corn-on-the-cob is held at Millersport?

A. Sweet Corn Festival.

———◆———

Q. Peter Falk starred as a manager for a girls' wrestling tag team in what 1980 movie filmed in Mahoning and Trumbull counties?

A. *All the Marbles.*

Q. "Red River Rock" was a hit by what group from Toledo?

A. Johnny and the Hurricanes.

———◆———

Q. In what 1952–55 television comedy did Cleveland native Jim Backus portray Judge Bradley Stevens?

A. "I Married Joan."

———◆———

Q. Cleveland and Akron hosted the filming of what 1980 motion picture starring Terri Garr and Raul Julia?

A. *The Escape Artist.*

———◆———

Q. In what community were the singing McGuire Sisters born?

A. Middletown.

———◆———

Q. What Akron-born actress starred as the romantic interest of Peter Gunn in the 1958–61 crime series?

A. Lola Albright.

———◆———

Q. Ohioan W. R. Burnett wrote what novel set in New York which became a 1950 film and later TV series by the same name?

A. *The Asphalt Jungle.*

———◆———

Q. What was Ohio-born Annie Oakley's full maiden name?

A. Phoebe Annie Oakley Mozee.

Q. What 1983 holiday film shot in Cleveland and Toronto starred Peter Billingsley and Darren McGavin?

A. *A Christmas Story.*

Q. Internationally known jazzman William Edward ("Wild Bill") Davison was born in what community?

A. Defiance.

Q. Ohioan Erma Bombeck became a regular on what early morning ABC television program?

A. "Good Morning America."

Q. What Toledo-born bass player accompanied such performers as Paul Anka, Gene Krupa, Vic Damone, and Judy Collins?

A. Bill Takas.

Q. Cleveland-born actress Debra Winger portrayed the character of Paula Pokrifki in what 1982 box office hit?

A. *An Officer and a Gentleman.*

Q. In 1985 what Paramount picture directed by Ron Howard was partially shot on location at Belmont County's Shadyside Stamping Plant?

A. *Gung Ho.*

Q. What Cincinnati-born newsman became executive vice president of NBC News in 1982?

A. Tom Pettit.

Q. Actor/dancer George Chakiris was born in what Ohio community?

A. Norwood.

Q. What great comedian has brought national fame to the ribs prepared at Montgomery Inn in suburban Cincinnati?

A. Bob Hope.

Q. Ohioan Catherine Gloria Balota became known by what stage name?

A. Kaye Ballard.

Q. What Columbus-born actor in over 120 movies played such roles as Billie Burke in *The Man Who Came to Dinner* and the Reverend Mr. Harper in *Arsenic and Old Lace?*

A. Grant Mitchell.

Q. Dayton native Tom Aldredge played what character on the CBS soap "The Guiding Light"?

A. Victor Kincaid.

Q. Jamie Farr starred in what 1983 television sitcom following his years on "M*A*S*H"?

A. "AfterMASH."

Q. In what television series did Tim Conway play the bumbling Ensign Chuck Parker?

A. "McHale's Navy."

Q. Corporal Klinger of TV's "M*A*S*H" would longingly refer to what Toledo eatery?

A. Tony Packo's Cafe.

———◆———

Q. In what 1973 Academy Award-winning film did Ohioan Paul Newman co-star with Robert Redford?

A. *The Sting*.

———◆———

Q. Lieutenant Dave Nelson was the character portrayed by what Cleveland-born actor in TV's crime-drama "VEGA$"?

A. Greg Morris.

———◆———

Q. What Dayton native founded the Dixieland Rhythm Kings in 1948?

A. Gene Mayl.

———◆———

Q. What 1948 film starring Peggy Cummins was partially shot in Lancaster?

A. *Green Grass of Wyoming*.

———◆———

Q. What Cleveland-born lyricist wrote such television theme songs as "Leave It to Beaver," "Restless Gun," "Tales of Wells Fargo," and "Lawrence Welk Champagne Time"?

A. Mort Greene.

———◆———

Q. In 1963 what Canton-born newsman was given credit as a behind-the-scenes negotiator, helping stop possible war during the Cuban missile crisis?

A. John Scali.

Q. Where was actress Catherine Bach born?

A. Warren.

———◆———

Q. Ohioan Lillian Gish starred in what movie recognized as the first modern feature motion picture?

A. *The Birth of a Nation* (1915).

———◆———

Q. What Akron-born actress portrayed Nancy Beebe, the manager of a fashionable Los Angeles restaurant, in the ABC sitcom "It's a Living"?

A. Marian Mercer.

———◆———

Q. In 1978 Hugh Downs became host of what ABC television series featuring investigative reporting?

A. "20/20."

———◆———

Q. Rhythm and blues singer Anita Baker was born in what Ohio city?

A. Toledo.

———◆———

Q. What Cleveland-born lead trumpeter played with Dizzy Gillespie and Lionel Hampton in the 1940s and Quincy Jones in 1959–60?

A. Benny Bailey.

———◆———

Q. Barbara Eden starred in what 1977 movie filmed in Lebanon?

A. *Harper Valley PTA.*

Q. What singing group, previously known as the Mascots, was formed in Canton in 1962?

A. The O'Jays.

Q. What Cleveland native was executive producer of such television hits as "Hogan's Heroes," "My Three Sons," "The Andy Griffith Show," and "M*A*S*H"?

A. Gene Reynolds.

Q. Talented director/writer/producer John Florea was born in what Ohio city?

A. Alliance.

Q. What Cleveland-born actor/director portrayed Ammen in the 1981 film *The Clash of the Titans?*

A. Burgess Meredith.

Q. Paul Newman made his screen debut in what film in 1955?

A. *The Silver Chalice.*

Q. What role did Cleveland-born actress Margaret Hamilton play in *The Wizard of Oz?*

A. The Wicked Witch of the West.

Q. What Zanesville-born character actor appeared in 220 movies and the television series "Fibber McGee and Molly"?

A. Addison Richards.

Q. What two Ohio-born writers were co-authors of the play "Shangri La" based on the novel *Lost Horizon?*

A. Jerome Lawrence and Robert E. Lee.

◆

Q. Screen star Lillian Gish was a native of what community?

A. Springfield.

◆

Q. What Oxford native was world famous for his standing performances playing boogie woogie piano?

A. John Rocco.

◆

Q. In 1979 Natalie Wood came to what city to film parts of ABC's *The Cracker Factory?*

A. Cleveland.

◆

Q. What fascinating attraction near Walnut Creek in Holmes County allows one to experience the Amish culture?

A. Amish House.

◆

Q. Who is music director of the Columbus Symphony Orchestra?

A. Alessandro Siciliani.

◆

Q. Where was television news personality Sander Vanocur born?

A. Cleveland.

Q. Xenia native Vic Dickenson became best known for his unique style on what instrument?

A. Trombone.

Q. Where was Ted Turner, owner/founder of the Cable News Network, born?

A. Cincinnati.

Q. In 1971 what Cleveland native received an Oscar for his screenplay *The French Connection?*

A. Ernest Tidyman.

Q. What Lima-born Big Band singer became a regular on the "Today" show from 1956 to 1958?

A. Helen O'Connell.

Q. Ohio began professional filmmaking in 1975 with what Columbia picture?

A. *Harry & Walter Go to New York.*

Q. What area in Cleveland, once known for its heavy industry, is now the city's primary entertainment district?

A. The Flats.

Q. For which movie did George Chakiris win an Oscar for Best Supporting Actor in 1961?

A. *West Side Story.*

Q. In what revolutionary three-dimensional motion picture concept did Lowell Thomas play a major role in the 1950s?

A. Cinerama.

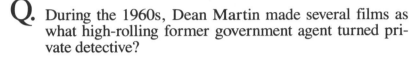

Q. During the 1960s, Dean Martin made several films as what high-rolling former government agent turned private detective?

A. Matt Helm.

Q. What Cleveland-born orchestra leader played the Los Angeles Coconut Grove from 1940 to 1970?

A. Freddy Martin.

Q. Jack Neuman, executive producer of such series as "A Man Called Shenandoah" and "Mr. Novak," was born in what city?

A. Toledo.

Q. Actress Sarah Jessica Parker of the TV series "Equal Justice" was born in what city?

A. Nelsonville.

Q. Noted jazz drummer Sonny Brown studied music at what Cincinnati high school?

A. Woodward High School.

Q. What Zanesville-born actor made his film debut in *Cry Wolf* (1945)?

A. Richard Basehart.

Q. What Akron native has appeared in such films as *That Lucky Touch, Just a Gigolo,* and *Looping?*

A. Sydne Rome.

Q. Where was veteran band leader Ted Lewis born?

A. Circleville.

Q. In what 1976–77 television series did Cincinnati native Mitchell Ryan star as Dan Walling, a corporate president?

A. "Executive Suite."

Q. Howard Hughes married what Canton-born actress in 1957?

A. Jean Peters.

Q. What famous actor/comedian was born in Holgate in 1892?

A. Joe E. Brown.

———◆———

Q. Willoughby-born art director Ted Haworth won an Oscar in 1957 for what movie?

A. *Sayonara.*

———◆———

Q. One of the last original floating theaters still in operation, what showboat is docked on the Ohio River in Cincinnati?

A. *Majestic.*

HISTORY

CHAPTER THREE

Q. During the Civil War what nine-year-old runaway from Newark became known in the North as the "drummer boy of Shiloh"?

A. Johnny Clem.

◆

Q. What household appliance was developed in 1907 by Murray Spangler while working as a night janitor at the Folwell Building in Canton?

A. Electric Suction Sweeper vacuum cleaner.

◆

Q. At what battle did "Mad Anthony" Wayne break the power of the Indian Confederation in 1794?

A. The Battle of Fallen Timbers.

◆

Q. Harry Stevans of Niles coined what great American culinary term for the frankfurters he served wrapped in a roll?

A. Hot dog.

◆

Q. In the fall of 1918, what automatic weapon was finally perfected at the Auto Ordnance shop in Cleveland?

A. Thompson submachine gun.

Q. To how many terms was Rutherford B. Hayes elected to serve as governor of Ohio?

A. Three.

Q. Who in 1669 is believed to have been the first European explorer to visit the Ohio area?

A. La Salle.

Q. Who pioneered Akron's rubber industry in 1870?

A. Dr. Benjamin Franklin Goodrich.

Q. Who in 1922 became the first woman in the nation to sit as a judge on a state supreme court?

A. Florence E. Allen.

Q. In 1967 what Clevelander became the first black elected mayor of a major American city?

A. Carl B. Stokes (Cleveland).

Q. What group organized in 1884 became a leading lobbying voice for union rights in Ohio?

A. Ohio Federation of Labor.

Q. John W. Hausserman, who maintained a summer home in New Richmond during the first part of the twentieth century, was known by what title?

A. "Gold King of the Philippines."

Q. How many U.S. presidents were born in Ohio?

A. Seven.

———◆———

Q. Cleveland led the nation in the installation of what type of traffic control devices on August 5, 1914?

A. Electric traffic signal lights.

———◆———

Q. What ardent abolitionist, who was convicted and hanged as a participant in the John Brown Harpers Ferry raid, is buried in Salem's Hope Cemetery?

A. Edwin Coppock.

———◆———

Q. How many miles of wagon trails existed in Ohio in 1803?

A. 1,030.

———◆———

Q. What movie star participated in the inauguration of the world's first air-rail service at Port Columbus Field on July 8, 1929?

A. Mary Pickford.

———◆———

Q. Distinguished eighteenth-century Shawnee chief Keigh-tugh-qua was known by what name to white settlers?

A. Cornstalk.

———◆———

Q. When constructed in 1812–14, what nine-story Ohio structure was the nation's tallest building west of the Atlantic seaboard?

A. Cincinnati Steam Mill.

Q. What campaign theme did William McKinley use to woo labor support in Ohio?

A. The "full dinner pail."

Q. Formed by Cincinnati printers, what became Ohio's first trade union in 1828?

A. Franklin Typographical Union.

Q. What Cleveland resident served as Woodrow Wilson's secretary of war?

A. Newton D. Baker.

Q. An unruly mob of some 12,000 spectators at an 1884 hanging caused the Ohio legislature to pass what law?

A. Privacy of executions law.

Q. In 1947, what U.S. senator from Ohio co-sponsored major legislation regarding labor relations?

A. Robert A. Taft (the Taft-Hartley Act).

Q. In 1917 the Morgan Engineering Company of Alliance perfected what munitions innovation?

A. The Gordon-Morgan disappearing gun carriage.

Q. How many Ohioans participated in the War of 1812?

A. 25,000.

Q. What revolutionary piece of photography equipment was patented on February 19, 1856, by Gambier resident H. L. Smith?

A. The tintype camera.

Q. What was the population of Ohio in 1810?

A. 230,760.

Q. Street cars made of what metal were first placed into service in Cleveland in 1926?

A. Aluminum.

Q. In 1763 what Ottawa chieftain unsuccessfully attempted to unite Indian tribes in Ohio country to wipe out the whites west of the Alleghenies?

A. Pontiac.

Q. In July of 1863, what daring Confederate thrust into Ohio resulted in the capture of over 2,000 Southern soldiers?

A. Morgan's Raid.

Q. Where was noted nineteenth-century financier Jay Cooke born in 1821?

A. Sandusky.

Q. Who served as president of Antioch College at Yellow Springs from 1853 to 1859?

A. Horace Mann.

Q. Prior to a clerical error made in his appointment to West Point, what was Ulysses Simpson Grant's name?

A. Hiram Ulysses Grant.

Q. What Ohio City resident made America's first automobile in 1891?

A. John Lambert.

Q. In 1811 what boat became the first steam-powered vessel on the waters of the Ohio River?

A. The *Orleans*.

Q. In what year was construction begun on the present Ohio capitol?

A. 1838 (dedicated January 6, 1857).

Q. What nickname was given to Mrs. Rutherford B. Hayes for not serving alcoholic drinks in the White House?

A. Lemonade Lucy.

Q. Homer was the childhood home of what 1872 Equal Rights Party presidential nominee?

A. Victoria Clafin Woodhull.

Q. What Ohio-born U.S. president was the only grandson of a person also elected president?

A. Benjamin Harrison.

Q. In 1914, what was the first U.S. city of over 100,000 to adopt a council–manager form of government?

A. Dayton.

Q. In 1911 Cincinnatian G. H. Lewis became the first person in the nation to be issued what type of license by the federal government?

A. Radio operator.

Q. What was the name of the cannon used by Major George Croghan and his 160 men to defend Fort Stephenson against overwhelming odds in August of 1813?

A. Old Betsy.

Q. Municipal suffrage rights were extended to the women of what Ohio city in 1917?

A. Columbus.

Q. What financial institution was founded by Mormon leader Joseph Smith to finance his Kirtland enterprises?

A. The Kirtland Safety Society anti-Bank-ing Company.

Q. In 1894 what Massillon resident led an army of unemployed workers to Washington, D.C., to protest poor economic conditions?

A. Jacob S. Coxey.

Q. Who founded the Diamond Match Company in 1880?

A. Ohio Columbus Barber.

Q. What dirigible broke apart in violent winds near Ava on September 3, 1925, killing Commander Zachary Lansdowne and thirteen crewmen?

A. The *Shenandoah*.

Q. Socialist Eugene V. Debs was arrested for violating the Espionage Act of 1917 after giving a speech in what Ohio city?

A. Canton, in 1918.

Q. How many miners lost their lives in the Millfield mine disaster of November 5, 1930?

A. Eighty-two.

Q. In pre–Civil War days, who was recognized as being Ohio's most notorious horse thief?

A. Shep Tinker.

Q. Who confronted Ohio in the "Toledo War" of 1835–36?
A. Michigan.

Q. What famous trial lawyer received his first job in 1878 at a Youngstown law office?

A. Clarence Darrow.

Q. What World War II submarine is on display at Cleveland?
A. U.S.S. *Cod*.

Q. During the 1940s and 1950s how many terms did Frank J. Lausche serve as governor of the state?

A. Five.

————◆————

Q. What kitchen appliance was first manufactured at Mansfield in 1955?

A. The electronic range.

————◆————

Q. What motto appeared on the Ohio state seal from 1866 to 1868?

A. *Imperium in Imperio* ("an empire within an empire").

————◆————

Q. As a teenager, what U.S. president drove mules as a towpath boy along the Ohio and Erie Canal?

A. James A. Garfield.

————◆————

Q. Where was the first 4-H CLub started by A. B. Graham in 1902?

A. Springfield.

————◆————

Q. What reward was placed on the head of the female Confederate spy Lottie Moon Clark of Oxford by the federal government?

A. $10,000, dead or alive.

————◆————

Q. What was the name of the nation's first shopping center that opened in Columbus in 1949?

A. Town and Country.

Q. In 1933, members of whose gang murdered the sheriff of Lima?

A. John Dillinger.

Q. Established in 1804 at Ames (now Amesville), the famous Coonskin Library received that name for what reason?

A. Pioneers purchased its books with animal skins.

Q. Benjamin Harrison, the twenty-third U.S. president, graduated from what Ohio college?

A. Miami University at Oxford.

Q. C. W. and F. A. Seiberling founded what company at Akron in 1898?

A. Goodyear Tire and Rubber Company.

Q. What Ohioan won the Miss America crown in 1978?

A. Susan Perkins.

Q. What was John Brown's occupation at Richfield during the early 1840s?

A. Wool broker and shepherd.

Q. What famous Ohio transportation firm failed in 1857 because of competition from the railroads?

A. The Ohio Stage Company.

Q. Prior to venturing into the vacuum cleaner business, H. W. Hoover owned what kind of firm in North Canton?

A. Harness and saddle manufacturing.

———◆———

Q. Whom did Virginia Governor Robert Dinwiddie send to the Ohio territory in 1753 in an attempt to dissuade further French colonization?

A. George Washington.

———◆———

Q. What unique canvas-clad begging sect camped near Plain City during the early part of the winter of 1816–17?

A. The Wandering Pilgrims.

———◆———

Q. The Ohio state legislature enacted what revenue-generating progam in 1971?

A. An income tax.

———◆———

Q. In 1843 what issue did the widow Tarbell use to incite local residents to ransack the Willoughby Medical College?

A. The disappearance of the deceased Mr. Tarbell from his grave.

———◆———

Q. Ohio Episcopalians founded what school of higher education in 1824?

A. Kenyon College.

———◆———

Q. Who was the heroine of the 1782 battle of Fort Henry (Virginia), now memorialized at Martins Ferry?

A. Elizabeth ("Betty") Zane.

Q. What candy was developed in 1912 by Cleveland resident Clarence Crane?

A. LifeSavers.

Q. The Patterson brothers of Dayton founded what manufacturing company in 1884?

A. National Cash Register Company.

Q. Who in 1749 traveled about the Ohio area burying lead markers on behalf of King Louis XV of France?

A. Celeron de Bienville.

Q. In the peak year of 1851 what was the total amount of toll revenues paid on the Miami and Erie Canal?

A. $351,897.

Q. What revolutionary automobile tire innovation was announced in Akron on May 11, 1947?

A. The tubeless tire.

Q. In 1858 what political action group became the first organization in the nation to endorse Abraham Lincoln for president?

A. The Richland County Lincoln Society.

Q. Who in 1866 founded a store in Strasburg that later received national recognition for its innovative merchandising?

A. Phillip A. Garver.

Q. Akron's American Cereal Company absorbed a competitive mill in Ravenna and adopted what new product trade name in 1886?

A. Quaker Oats.

Q. The devastating floods of 1913 took how many lives in Ohio?

A. 430.

Q. Seneca John, chief of the Senecas, was executed in 1828 for what crime against his brother, Cornstalk?

A. "Witchcraft murder."

Q. What Revolutionary War general, an organizer of the Ohio Company, established the first white settlement in Ohio?

A. Rufus Putnam.

Q. What U.S. president was born in Delaware, Ohio, on October 4, 1822?

A. Rutherford B. Hayes.

Q. In what year was prohibition legislation enacted in Ohio?

A. 1918.

Q. What was the first railroad chartered in Ohio?

A. Mad River and Lake Erie Railroad (1832).

Q. As a U.S. senator, what Cincinnati native sponsored the 1883 act which created the U.S. civil service system?

A. George Hunt Pendleton (the Pendleton Act).

Q. At Milford, who became the country's first female police chief in 1914?

A. Dolly Spencer.

Q. On what date was Ohio admitted to the Union as a state?

A. March 1, 1803.

Q. What Ohio-born U.S. president possessed the ability to write simultaneously in Greek and Latin?

A. James A. Garfield.

Q. What was the first steel plant to operate in Youngstown?

A. Union Iron & Steel Company (1892).

Q. What commodity was flown from Dayton to Columbus on the first air freight flight in 1910?

A. Silk (seventy pounds).

Q. How many of Toledo's ten banks closed their doors during the Great Depression?

A. Seven.

Q. What Mohawk Indian leader, born in Ohio country in 1742, became a colonel in the British Army?

A. Thayendanegea, or Joseph Brant.

Q. In what year did Ohio voters approve changing the gubernatorial term from two to four years?

A. 1959.

Q. Where did the nation's first junior high school open in 1909?

A. Columbus.

Q. Where was the nation's first single-course concrete pavement laid in 1891?

A. Bellefontaine.

Q. During the Civil War, what Cincinnati firm supplied all the soap for the Union army?

A. Procter and Gamble.

Q. In 1964 the U.S. Supreme Court made what ruling with regard to Ohio's house of representatives?

A. Reapportionment was to be based on population.

Q. What college was established in 1876 with funding from an $80,000-endowment from the Atwood estate of tavern owner Nehemiah Atwood?

A. Rio Grande College.

Q. Who commanded the band of cutthroats who butchered ninety-six unarmed Christian Indians at Gnadenhutten in 1782?

A. Captain David Williamson.

———◆———

Q. What unusual style of bridges was used on the National Road in the eastern part of the state?

A. S-bridges.

———◆———

Q. What Ohioan established himself as the first billionaire in the United States?

A. John D. Rockefeller.

———◆———

Q. During World War I, Goodyear Tire and Rubber Company trained hundreds of pilots to handle what type of lighter-than-air craft at its Wingfoot Lake development near Suffield?

A. Small dirigibles and observation balloons.

———◆———

Q. What was James A. Garfield's occupation while attending Hiram College?

A. School janitor.

———◆———

Q. What railroad union local was established in Cincinnati in 1855?

A. Brotherhood of Locomotive Engineers.

———◆———

Q. What ethnic group set up the nation's first kindergarten in Columbus in 1838?

A. German.

Q. What Cleveland automobile company on July 30, 1898, became the first in the nation to run an automobile advertisement?

A. Winton Motor Car Company.

———◆———

Q. On December 10, 1886, who was elected the first president of the newly formed American Federation of Trade and Labor?

A. Samuel Gompers (at Columbus).

———◆———

Q. Through what act did the United States formally take possession of the Ohio country?

A. The Land Ordinance of 1785.

———◆———

Q. What was the name of the country's first railroad car chapel, dedicated at Cincinnati on May 23, 1891?

A. Evangel.

———◆———

Q. What was the average speed of craft on Ohio's barge system in the 1830s and 1840s?

A. Two to three miles per hour.

———◆———

Q. In 1885 who became the first person hanged at the Ohio State Penitentiary?

A. Valentine Wagner.

———◆———

Q. What naval commander stated after the Battle of Lake Erie, "We have met the enemy, and they are ours"?

A. Oliver Hazard Perry.

Q. A leaky gas main severely damaged what nearly completed government building in Columbus on April 14, 1932?

A. The Ohio Departments of State Building.

Q. What was the minimum annual attendance requirement for public school students under legislation passed in 1877?

A. Twelve weeks.

Q. In 1926 what Canton newspaper editor noted for exposing organized crime was murdered by racketeers?

A. Don Mellett.

Q. What Columbian made aviation history as the first woman to fly solo around the world?

A. Jerrie L. Mock.

Q. What celebrated Civil War cannon at Charleston Harbor was cast from iron of the Hecla region?

A. The Swamp Angel.

Q. In the summer of 1883 three days of fighting between the people of Cincinnati and the state militia left the courthouse burned and how many persons killed or wounded?

A. Over 300.

Q. Which Ohio-born president owned a newspaper in Marion?

A. Warren G. Harding.

Q. What mammoth structure measuring 1,175 feet in length, 325 feet in width, and 221 feet in height with no interior supports, was completed at Akron in 1929?

A. The Goodyear Zeppelin Airdock.

Q. What do Charles J. Guiteau and Leon F. Czolgosz have in common?

A. Each assassinated an Ohio-born president (Guiteau, Garfield; Czolgosz, McKinley).

Q. From what prison did Confederate General John Morgan and six of his riders tunnel their way to freedom?

A. The Ohio Penitentiary (Columbus).

Q. Approximately how many one-room schoolhouses did Ohio have during the late eighteenth and early nineteenth centuries?

A. 11,000.

Q. By what margin of electoral votes did Ohioan Rutherford Birchard Hayes win his presidential bid?

A. One.

Q. What Massachusetts-born Ohioan in 1833 patented a mechanical reaper one year before McCormick's famous invention?

A. Obed Hussey.

Q. In what city did a July 23, 1968, shoot-out leave three policemen, three black militants, and one bystander dead and fifteen other persons wounded?

A. Cleveland.

Q. What early Worthington resident printed and issued paper money in the denominations of 6¼¢ 12½¢, 25¢, 50¢, $1, and $2?

A. Captain Ezra Griswold.

◆

Q. What 1804 grist mill at Garrettsville is powered by the world's largest water wheel?

A. Hopkins Old Water Mill.

◆

Q. To date, what Ohioan is the only former U.S. president to be named a U.S. Supreme Court justice?

A. William Howard Taft.

◆

Q. What U.S. president, born in Virginia, was living in Ohio when elected?

A. William Henry Harrison.

◆

Q. For what does the company name *Delco* stand?

A. Dayton Engineering Laboratories Company.

◆

Q. What fortress constructed at the Marietta settlement in 1788 provided protection from Indians?

A. Campus Martius.

◆

Q. Who invented a sheet-steel road scraper and established a plant for its manufacture at Sidney in 1879?

A. Benjamin Slusser.

Q. What Cincinnati native became the first woman awarded a General Motors dealership in a major metropolitan area?

A. Marge Schott.

Q. What was Ohio's first recorded manufacturing endeavor, established at Cincinnati in 1793?

A. A tannery.

Q. What was the bottom pay scale for common laborers who constructed the Miami and Erie Canal?

A. Five dollars per month.

Q. Where was the Miner's National Association formed in 1873?

A. Youngstown.

Q. What Ohio aristocrat helped finance Aaron Burr's plans to create an empire in the southwest?

A. Harman Blennerhassett.

Q. The state militia was sent to what two cities to restore order during the great railroad labor riots of 1877?

A. Newark and Cincinnati.

Q. Because of its impregnability, Fort Meigs earned what title during the War of 1812?

A. The Gibraltar of the Northwest.

Q. How many inmates died in the April 21, 1930, fire at the Ohio penitentiary at Columbus?

A. 322.

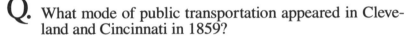

Q. Charles F. Kettering developed what revolutionary automotive device in a Dayton woodshed in 1909?

A. The automobile self-starter.

Q. What community served as the capital of Ohio from 1810 to 1812?

A. Zanesville.

Q. What mode of public transportation appeared in Cleveland and Cincinnati in 1859?

A. Horse-drawn trolleys.

Q. Opened in 1773 for Indian children by Moravian missionaries, the first school begun in Ohio country was in what town?

A. Schoenbrunn.

Q. Under what name was Ohio State University established at Columbus in 1870?

A. Ohio Agricultural and Mechanical College.

Q. What Coshoctan-born labor leader became president of the AFL in 1924?

A. William Green.

Q. What nickname was given Cincinnati in the 1850s because of its prominence in the meat packing industry?

A. "Porkopolis."

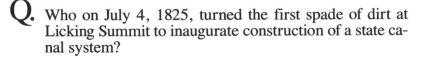

Q. Who on July 4, 1825, turned the first spade of dirt at Licking Summit to inaugurate construction of a state canal system?

A. Dewitt Clinton, governor of New York.

Q. What type of postal delivery equipment was first made at Cleveland in 1899?

A. An automobile mail wagon.

Q. Traveling from Buffalo to Detroit via Cleveland and Sandusky, what craft in 1818 became the first steam-powered boat on Lake Erie?

A. *Walk-in-the-Water*.

Q. During World War I the Wright Airplane Company of Dayton shipped how many DeHaviland aircraft to France?

A. 4,587.

Q. Where was black orator Sojourner Truth's famous "Ain't I a Woman" speech made?

A. Akron.

Q. How many enlisted men did Ohio provide to the Union army during the Civil War?

A. 340,000.

Q. In 1834 Dr. William G. Thompson's factory in Zanesville was the first in the United States to produce what "hot" item?

A. Lucifer matches.

───◆───

Q. What Ohioan became the first president general of the Daughters of the American Revolution?

A. Caroline Scott Harrison (wife of President Benjamin Harrison).

───◆───

Q. What great five-masted schooner was launched at Toledo on April 21, 1881?

A. The *David Dows*.

───◆───

Q. Demanding higher wages and a ten-hour work day, what union in 1836 became the first to go on strike in Ohio?

A. The Cincinnati Harnessmakers Union.

───◆───

Q. What Cadiz resident served as the American minister to Japan from 1873 to 1885?

A. John A. Bingham.

───◆───

Q. What religious sect began migrating into the Killduck and Tuscarawas valleys in 1807?

A. Amish.

───◆───

Q. Who in 1751 founded a Catholic settlement among the Huron Indians near present-day Sandusky?

A. Father De La Richardie.

Q. In 1778 Shawnee Indians held what noted frontiersman captive in Et-Nah Woods near the Seven Caves area?

A. Daniel Boone.

———◆———

Q. Who began manufacturing automobiles in Warren in 1899?

A. J. Ward Packard.

———◆———

Q. The arrival of what packet craft at Massillon signaled the opening of the first phase of the Ohio and Erie Canal?

A. The *Allen Trimble*.

———◆———

Q. What pro-prohibition organization was formed at Hillsboro in December of 1873?

A. The Women's Temperance Crusade.

———◆———

Q. How many Ohio banks failed during the great panic of 1837?

A. Nine.

———◆———

Q. Who opened Ohio's first commercial brewery in Cincinnati in 1806?

A. James Dover.

———◆———

Q. What "super highway" opened across the northern part of Ohio in 1955?

A. The Ohio Turnpike.

Q. What Clevelander patented the ice cream cone-rolling machine on January 29, 1924?

A. C. R. Taylor.

———◆———

Q. How many Ohioans have served as vice presidents of the United States?

A. Three (Thomas A. Hendricks, Charles W. Fairbanks, and Charles C. Dawes).

———◆———

Q. What unionists' political party was organized in Columbus in 1872?

A. The Labor Reform Party.

———◆———

Q. How many miles of commercial canals were constructed in Ohio from 1825 to 1847?

A. 813.

———◆———

Q. In 1903 what right was restored to the governor of Ohio after over one hundred years of not having it?

A. The right to veto legislation.

———◆———

Q. John W. Bricker, who served Ohio as governor and as a United States senator, ran for what national office on the Republican ticket in 1944?

A. Vice president of the United States.

———◆———

Q. What religious movement swept the Ohio Valley from 1797 to 1804?

A. The Great Revival (or Great Awakening).

Q. Ohio State University pioneered what communication first in the nation in 1922?

A. Created WOSU, the first educational radio station.

———◆———

Q. Guidelines set by the state constitution of 1850 called for state officials to be selected by what means?

A. Popular election.

———◆———

Q. Who served as the first governor of the Northwest Territory?

A. General Arthur St. Clair.

———◆———

Q. Who founded a glass plant at Rossford in 1896?

A. Edward Ford.

———◆———

Q. What Ohio Democrat ran unsuccessfully for president in 1920 with Franklin D. Roosevelt as his running mate?

A. James Middleton Cox.

———◆———

Q. What union organization founded an orphanage at Tiffin in 1897?

A. The Order of United American Mechanics.

———◆———

Q. The statue of what former Ohio governor represents the state in the Statuary Hall of the U.S. Capitol in Washington, D.C.?

A. William Allen (governor, 1874–76).

Q. What notable 1858 Ohio court case freed thirty-seven residents charged with violating the Fugitive Slave Law?

A. The Oberlin-Wellington rescue case.

———◆———

Q. Economic problems, a banking law conviction, and rumors of impending arrest led to the flight of what religious empire-builder from Ohio?

A. Joseph Smith.

———◆———

Q. What 1795 treaty brought a formal end to Indian warfare in Ohio country?

A. The Treaty of Greenville.

———◆———

Q. Historian Ickabod Flewellen established what ethnic museum in Cleveland in 1956?

A. Afro-American Cultural and Historical Museum.

———◆———

Q. By 1849 how many boats were working the Ohio River?

A. 2,492.

———◆———

Q. What 1934 strike at Toledo received national attention as the first major strike in the automobile industry?

A. The Auto-Lite strike.

Q. What influential national legislation was authored in 1890 by a Lancaster-born senator, brother of a Civil War general?

A. Sherman Antitrust Act (Sen. John Sherman, brother of General William T. Sherman).

Q. What Steubenville native served as President Abraham Lincoln's secretary of war?

A. Edwin Stanton.

Q. The Baltimore and Ohio Railroad was the first line in the nation to provide what creature comfort for passengers traveling in hot weather?

A. Air-conditioned cars.

Q. Who laid out Akron in 1825?

A. General Simon Perkins of Warren.

Q. What 1748 real estate venture organized by Virginians attempted to colonize 500,000 acres of Ohio territory?

A. The Ohio Land Company.

Q. Established at Dayton in 1813, what became Ohio's first recorded workers' organization?

A. The Dayton Mechanics' Society.

Q. What nineteenth-century Geneva resident created a penmanship system and founded business schools in over forty cities?

A. Platt R. Spencer.

Q. What fort was built in 1789 at the present site of Cincinnati?

A. Fort Washington.

Q. What cult leader arrived on the banks of Leatherwood Creek near Salesville in 1828 and declared himself to be God?

A. Joseph Dylkes.

＋

Q. In 1835, what action by Pres. Andrew Jackson avoided actual fighting between the state of Ohio and the territory of Michigan?

A. He sent agents to persuade the governors to accept a truce until Congress could settle the border dispute.

＋

Q. What was the train fare in 1853 for the eleven-hour, 254-mile trip between Cincinnati and Cleveland?

A. Seven dollars.

＋

Q. Where did the Industrial Workers of the World, known as Wobblies, first strike in Ohio?

A. Youngstown (1905).

＋

Q. In what year was the State Bank of Ohio established?
A. 1846.

＋

Q. In 1933 the voters of Ohio embraced what proposal for assistance to the elderly?

A. Old-age pension law.

＋

Q. What 1805 post road stretched westward from Wheeling to Kentucky via Zanesville, Lancaster, and Chillicothe?

A. Zane's Trace.

Q. What organization was formed at Ohio State University in 1928 to honor outstanding Ohio journalists?

A. Ohio Journalism Hall of Fame.

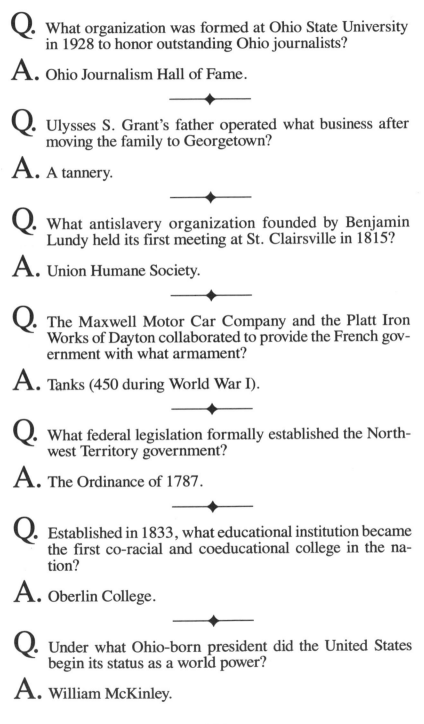

Q. Ulysses S. Grant's father operated what business after moving the family to Georgetown?

A. A tannery.

Q. What antislavery organization founded by Benjamin Lundy held its first meeting at St. Clairsville in 1815?

A. Union Humane Society.

Q. The Maxwell Motor Car Company and the Platt Iron Works of Dayton collaborated to provide the French government with what armament?

A. Tanks (450 during World War I).

Q. What federal legislation formally established the Northwest Territory government?

A. The Ordinance of 1787.

Q. Established in 1833, what educational institution became the first co-racial and coeducational college in the nation?

A. Oberlin College.

Q. Under what Ohio-born president did the United States begin its status as a world power?

A. William McKinley.

Q. What young Bavarian immigrant is credited with displaying America's first Christmas tree at Wooster in 1847?

A. August Imgard.

Q. In 1866 Columbus unionists formed what organization to press for a shorter work day?

A. The Eight-Hour League.

Q. What railroad line joined with the Mad River and Lake Erie line in 1846 to form the first complete north to south line across the state?

A. Little Miami Railroad.

Q. What Ohio institution of higher learning became the first municipal university in the nation in 1870?

A. The University of Cincinnati.

Q. What amount of tax was first levied in 1825 for support of Ohio schools?

A. One-half mill tax.

Q. Who introduced Methodism to the Wyandot Indians in northwestern Ohio in the early 1800s?

A. John Stewart.

Q. What state law enforcement agency was established in November of 1933?

A. The State Highway Patrol.

Q. In 1926 building zoning was upheld for the first time by the U.S. Supreme Court because of a case in what Ohio city?

A. Euclid.

Q. What Clyde resident was commander of the Army of the Tennessee during the Civil War?

A. Brigadier General James Birdseye McPherson.

Q. Capital University was established by what religious group in 1850?

A. Lutherans.

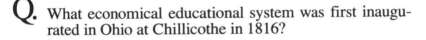

Q. During the Civil War what Dayton resident became the leader of the Peace Democrats party, or Copperheads?

A. Clement L. Vallandigham.

Q. What economical educational system was first inaugurated in Ohio at Chillicothe in 1816?

A. The Lancastrian system.

Q. In 1873 what farm political movement established itself in Ohio?

A. The Ohio Grange.

Q. What Canfield resident served as comptroller of the U.S. Treasury under both the Taylor and Lincoln administrations?

A. Elisha Whittlesey.

Q. What Revolutionary War hero referred to the city as the "eighth wonder of the world" while visiting Cincinnati in 1825?

A. General Lafayette.

＋

Q. Under what name was the first private school in Ohio country founded at Marietta in 1797?

A. Muskingum Academy.

＋

Q. What Ohioan served as vice president under President Theodore Roosevelt?

A. Charles W. Fairbanks.

＋

Q. In 1959 Ashtabula, Cleveland, Conneaut, Fairport, Huron, Lorain, Sandusky, and Toledo all became ports of what waterway?

A. The St. Lawrence Seaway.

＋

Q. What tribe of Indians was characterized as the most hostile in Ohio in the 1700s?

A. The Shawnees.

＋

Q. Where was the first cook stove in Madison County installed in the late 1830s?

A. The Red Brick Tavern, Lafayette.

＋

Q. In 1761 what Moravian missionary established a mission in what became Tuscarawas County?

A. Christian Frederick Post.

Q. What noted nineteenth-century political orator was a resident of Tiffin?

A. General William H. Gibson.

Q. Ohio-born President Rutherford B. Hayes and wife, Lucy, introduced what springtime custom at the White House enjoyed by children today?

A. Easter Egg rolling on the White House lawn.

Q. From 1812 to 1816 what city served as the seat of Ohio government?

A. Chillicothe.

Q. In what Ohio city in 1868 did the nation's railroad conductors form a national brotherhood?

A. Columbus.

Q. What two watch manufacturing firms located plants in Canton in 1888?

A. Hampden Watch Manufacturing Company and Duebar Watch Company.

Q. Who was the first Ohio governor to promote building a canal system in the state?

A. Ethan Allen Brown.

Q. Under what name was Hiram College founded in 1850 by the Disciples of Christ?

A. The Western Reserve Eclectic Institute.

Q. By 1930 what percentage of Ohioans were farmers by occupation?

A. 15.1 percent.

------◆------

Q. Who served as governor of Ohio from 1822 to 1826?

A. Jeremiah Marrow.

------◆------

Q. Little Turtle was a famous chief of what Indian tribe in western Ohio in the 1700s?

A. The Miamis.

------◆------

Q. What Ohio-born president was the first to have his mother attend his inauguration?

A. James A. Garfield.

------◆------

Q. What theological school was founded by the Presbyterians in 1829?

A. Lane Theological Seminary.

------◆------

Q. As an Indian captive, who in 1755 probably was the first white man to live on the site of present-day Elyria?

A. Colonel James Smith.

------◆------

Q. How many public high schools were there in Ohio in 1860?

A. Fifty.

ARTS & LITERATURE

C H A P T E R   F O U R

Q. In 1848 what song composed by Stephen Foster in Cincinnati took the nation by storm?

A. "Oh! Susanna."

Q. Zane Grey, who was born in Zanesville, pursued what profession prior to becoming a novelist?

A. Dentistry.

Q. What 1952 book gained Norman Vincent Peale national recognition?

A. *The Power of Positive Thinking*.

Q. What Sandusky-born theater magnate lost his life on the *Lusitania*?

A. Charles Frohman.

Q. Where was America's first presidential library established?

A. Fremont (the Rutherford B. Hayes Library, 1916).

Q. What Highland County native drew the comic strip *Terry and the Pirates?*

A. Milton Caniff.

————◆————

Q. During the 1830s, what noted showboat troupe working out of Cincinnati brought Shakespearean plays to people on the Ohio River?

A. The Chapman family.

————◆————

Q. What respected Dayton-born musician collaborated with Duke Ellington on hundreds of compositions, including "Suite Thursday" and the adaptation of "Nutcracker Suite"?

A. Billy ("Swee' Pea") Strayhorn.

————◆————

Q. The Stocker Fine Arts Center is on what Elyria college campus?

A. Lorain County Community College.

————◆————

Q. Who served as conductor of the Cincinnati Symphony Orchestra from 1909 to 1912?

A. Leopold Stokowski.

————◆————

Q. In 1920 what theatrical organization became the first black dramatic group in the state?

A. The Gilpin Players.

————◆————

Q. Where was watercolorist Charles Burchfield born?

A. Ashtabula.

Q. In what short story did Columbus-born author James Thurber write of a man who daydreams to find relief from his nagging wife?

A. "The Secret Life of Walter Mitty."

Q. Where is the Southeastern Ohio Symphony Orchestra headquartered?

A. New Concord.

Q. What was the first newspaper to be published in the village of Cleveland?

A. The *Register* (in 1818).

Q. What Cincinnati-born author penned the highly acclaimed novel *Cannon Hill* in 1949?

A. Mary Margaret Deasy.

Q. What became the official state song October 14, 1969?

A. "Beautiful Ohio."

Q. Why was the Columbus Theater closed by the city in 1843?

A. It was declared a public nuisance.

Q. During what month is the annual downtown Arts Festival held in Findlay?

A. June.

Q. What former station on the Underground Railroad is reputedly the place where Eliza in *Uncle Tom's Cabin* found refuge after crossing the Ohio River on ice?

A. Rankin House, in Ripley.

Q. What was the name of the first minstrel show troupe to be organized in Ohio?

A. Virginia Minstrels.

Q. *Portrait of an Election: The 1980 Presidential Campaign* was the fourth book written by what Ohio-born author?

A. Elizabeth Drew.

Q. What widely read magazine of general interest to children is published in Columbus?

A. *Highlights for Children*.

Q. George Wesley Bellows, who was greatly responsible for the revival of lithography as an art form in this country, was born in what Ohio city in 1882?

A. Columbus.

Q. What 1796 book was the first published in Ohio country?

A. *Maxwell's Code*.

Q. What opera house is home for the Dayton Ballet and the Contemporary Dance Company?

A. The Victory Theater.

Q. While serving a five-year sentence at the Ohio State Penitentiary, author William Sydney Porter created what famous pen name?

A. O. Henry.

Q. What Dayton native was the first black American writer to receive international recognition?

A. Paul Laurence Dunbar.

Q. The McMicken School of Design was opened in Cincinnati in 1869 by what art instructor?

A. Charles T. Webber.

Q. Bruce Catton, who won the 1953 Pulitzer Prize for *A Stillness at Appomattox,* attended what Ohio college?

A. Oberlin.

Q. What Jewish publication was established in Cincinnati in 1854?

A. *American Israelite.*

Q. What is the only remaining opera house in Butler County?

A. Sorg Opera House, Middletown.

Q. Because of his critical style of writing, what nickname was given to Meigs County native Ambrose Bierce?

A. Bitter Bierce.

Q. What Mount Vernon native composed "I Wish I Was in Dixie," "Turkey in the Straw," and "Old Dan Tucker"?

A. Daniel ("Dan") Emmett.

Q. What award-winning Ohioan penned the novel *Who Is Teddy Villanova?*

A. Thomas Berger.

Q. The nation's first color comic supplement was created in 1894 by what cartoonist from Lancaster?

A. Richard Fenton Outcault.

Q. What Pulitzer Prize-winning novelist from Mansfield is known for such works as *The Green Bay Tree, Early Autumn,* and *The Farm?*

A. Louis Bromfield.

Q. What famous American poet called Cincinnati the "Queen of the West"?

A. Henry Wadsworth Longfellow.

Q. The magazine *MS* was founded in 1972 by what Toledo-born feminist and writer?

A. Gloria Steinem.

Q. What Portsmouth native was the first musician to make successful use of an electrically amplified violin?

A. Hezekiah Leroy Gordon Smith.

Q. What Ohioan composed numerous hymns including "Softly and Tenderly" (1880) and "Jesus Is All the World to Me" (1904)?

A. William Leland Thompson.

Q. Yellow Springs native Virginia Hamilton received a Newbery Award in 1975 for what children's book?

A. *M. C. Higgins, the Great.*

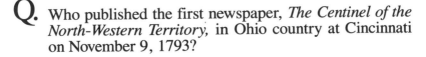

Q. What Youngstown art museum is devoted solely to American art?

A. Butler Institute of American Art.

Q. In what year was the Cleveland Symphony Orchestra founded?

A. 1918.

Q. Who published the first newspaper, *The Centinel of the North-Western Territory,* in Ohio country at Cincinnati on November 9, 1793?

A. William Maxwell.

Q. For what book is Ohioan Ruth McKenney best known?

A. *My Sister Eileen.*

Q. The Negro spiritual "Nobody Knows de Trouble I've Seen" was written by what Ohioan?

A. Clarence Cameron White.

Q. *Motherhood: The Second Oldest Profession* was written by what Ohio author?

A. Erma Bombeck.

Q. What artist painted the *Battle of Lake Erie*, which hangs in the Ohio state capitol?

A. William H. Powell.

Q. By what name was Kelleys Island portrayed in Walter Havighurst's 1949 novel *Signature of Time?*

A. Hazard Island.

Q. At age fourteen what award-winning jazz pianist was the featured soloist with the Toledo Youth Orchestra?

A. Stanley A. Cowell.

Q. Sherwood Anderson is best remembered for what work describing life in a small Ohio community?

A. *Winesburg, Ohio* (1919).

Q. Who opened the first art school in Ohio at Cincinnati in 1826?

A. Frederick Eckstein.

Q. What was the first drama ever performed in Columbus, in April of 1828?

A. *She Stoops to Conquer.*

Q. While teaching at Kenyon College, what poet/critic founded the prestigious literary magazine *Kenyon Review* and edited it from 1939 to 1958?

A. John Crowe Ransom.

◆

Q. What Springfield native received the Writers Guild of America award for the best screen play of 1963 for *The Great Escape?*

A. William Riley Burnett.

◆

Q. In 1826 what newspaper became the first daily west of Philadelphia?

A. *Cincinnati Commercial Register*.

◆

Q. James Albert Wales, who served as cartoonist for *Puck* magazine and helped found *Judge* magazine, was born in what Ohio community?

A. Clyde.

◆

Q. What Zanesville-born designer/architect created such works as the Woolworth Building in Chicago and the U.S. Supreme Court Building?

A. Cass Gilbert.

◆

Q. What Garrettsville-born poet is best known for his 1930 work "The Bridge"?

A. Hart Crane.

◆

Q. What uniquely designed Rossford studio allows people to watch glass being blown?

A. Blackstone Art Studio.

Q. "Down by the Old Mill Stream" was penned by what Findlay composer?

A. Tell Taylor.

Q. What Ohio city furnished Harriet Beecher Stowe with the characters she used in *Uncle Tom's Cabin?*

A. Cincinnati.

Q. What Cincinnati *Enquirer* staffer won the 1991 Pulitzer Prize for editorial cartooning?

A. Jim Borgman.

Q. Who founded the abolitionist newspaper *The Philanthropist* at Cincinnati in 1836, only to later have his press destroyed by a proslavery mob?

A. James G. Birney.

Q. Upon arrival from England in 1819, in what Ohio community did the great landscape painter Thomas Cole settle with his parents?

A. Steubenville.

Q. The opera *Voodoo* was composed by what Ohioan?

A. Henry Lawrence Freeman.

Q. Stephen Birmingham wrote what highly acclaimed book on upper-class black families?

A. *Certain People*.

Q. Who designed the Ohio state flag?

A. Architect John Eisemann.

Q. Though born in Knoxville, Tennessee, what contemporary American black poet has long been a resident of Cincinnati?

A. Nikki Giovanni.

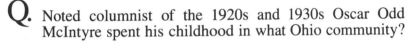

Q. What Lima-born tenor sax player is best known for his lengthy, descriptive improvisations?

A. Joe Henderson.

Q. Noted columnist of the 1920s and 1930s Oscar Odd McIntyre spent his childhood in what Ohio community?

A. Gallipolis.

Q. What Columbus-born historian has won two Pulitzer prizes, one for history and one for biography?

A. Arthur M. Schlesinger, Jr.

Q. The story of what famous Indian chief is told in an outdoor drama at the Sugarloaf Mountain Amphitheater near Chillicothe?

A. Tecumseh.

Q. In 1967 what Ohio State University student took his winning band to the National American College Jazz Festival?

A. Ladd McIntosh.

Q. With what work did Cleveland painter Archibald M. Willard achieve much national recognition in the 1870s?

A. *The Spirit of '76.*

Q. The *Western Intelligencer* newspaper was founded in 1811 to promote what community as the site of state government?

A. Worthington.

Q. The hymn "Nearer Home" was written by what Hamilton County native?

A. Phoebe Cary.

Q. *Tar, a Midwest Childhood,* written in 1926, was the fictional story of the life of what famous Camden-born author?

A. Sherwood Anderson.

Q. Who in 1886 organized the nation's most famous and enduring minstrel troupe that had headquarters in Columbus?

A. Al G. Field.

Q. What pro-abolitionist publication was headquartered in Salem?

A. *The Anti-Slavery Bugle.*

Q. What Springfield-born trombonist toured with Quincy Jones in *Free and Easy,* 1959–60?

A. Quentin Leonard ("Butter") Jackson.

Q. The poem "The Negro Speaks of Rivers" was written by what poet the summer after his graduation from high school in Cleveland?

A. Langston Hughes.

Q. W. R. Burnett's novel *Asphalt Jungle* has been published in how many languages?

A. Twelve.

Q. What famous painter, most recognized for his work *Whistling Boy,* spent his last years teaching painting in Cincinnati?

A. Frank Duveneck.

Q. Wartime hysteria brought about the resignation of what German conductor from the Cincinnati Symphony Orchestra in 1917?

A. Dr. Ernst Kunwald.

Q. In 1911 Ambrose G. Bierce wrote what well-known work displaying his wit and cynical style?

A. *The Devil's Dictionary.*

Q. What is the name of Columbus's professional repertory ballet company?

A. Ballet Metropolitan.

Q. In what city did William Holmes McGuffey compile his first *Eclectic Reader?*

A. Oxford.

Q. Who is credited with utilizing the blackface technique in Ohio theater as early as 1823?

A. Edwin Forrest.

Q. What Lorain-born author won the 1988 Pulitzer Prize for the novel *Beloved?*

A. Toni Morrison.

Q. Established in 1972, what Cincinnati facility consisting of two theaters, three galleries, and classrooms is noted for displaying the work of minority artists?

A. Arts Consortium.

Q. What novelist and four-time mayor of Toledo was born in Urbana?

A. Brand Whitlock.

Q. What became the first college music department in the nation in 1865?

A. The Oberlin Conservatory of Music.

Q. What Wilmington-born reedman/flutist played in the pit band for the hit Broadway musical *Raisin?*

A. Norris William Turney.

Q. First published in the late 1820s, what was the first labor newspaper published in Ohio?

A. *Working Man's Shield.*

Q. What Ohio art museum displays the Severance collection of arms and armor?

A. The Cleveland Museum of Art.

Q. The statue of Abraham Lincoln in Cincinnati's Lytle Park is the work of what sculptor?

A. George Grey Barnard.

Q. What syndicated newspaper column brought Norman Vincent Peale national popularity?

A. "Confident Living."

Q. Marysville resident Otway Curry composed what theme song for William Henry Harrison's 1840 presidential campaign?

A. "Log Cabin Song."

Q. In 1946 Springfield-born Lois Lenski received the coveted Newbery Medal for what children's book?

A. *Strawberry Girl.*

Q. What Cleveland-born saxophonist composed *Ghosts,* said to have been the anthem of 1960s black music?

A. Albert Ayler.

Q. Opening in 1850, what was Toledo's first theater?

A. Union Hall.

Q. What composer from Oxford wrote scores for *Ben Hur* and *Macbeth?*

A. Edgar Stillman Kelley.

———◆———

Q. What sculptor created the statues of William Henry Harrison, Henry Clay, and Winfield Scott for the capitol at Columbus?

A. Thomas D. Jones.

———◆———

Q. In 1836 the *Cincinnati Gazette* installed what innovative new piece of equipment?

A. An Adams automated press.

———◆———

Q. By what term were shaped musical notes identified by early Ohio pioneers?

A. Buckwheat notes.

———◆———

Q. What Dover artist hand-carved out of a solid piece of walnut the Plier Tree containing 511 interconnecting pairs of working pliers?

A. Ernest ("Mooney") Warther.

———◆———

Q. Known as Whistler's favorite student, what great American etcher was born in Cleveland in 1856?

A. Otto Bacher.

———◆———

Q. What Madison cartoonist created such strip characters as Happy Hooligan, Maud, and Alphonse and Gaston?

A. Frederick Burr Opper.

Q. Where is the Blossom Music Center situated?

A. Cuyahoga Falls.

Q. Bible era artifacts from the Near East and Jewish histori-cal art and memorabilia are a part of what Cincinnati dis-play?

A. Gallery of Art and Artifacts of the Hebrew Union Col-lege.

Q. What Cincinnati-born novelist became drama critic for *Time* magazine?

A. Louis Kronenberger.

Q. In the Garst Museum at Greenville, a painting by what artist depicts the signing of the Treaty of Greenville in 1795?

A. Howard Chandler Christy.

Q. What cartoon character created by Kin Hubbard of Belle-fontaine was syndicated both nationally and internation-ally?

A. Abe Martin.

Q. What Mount Vernon resident organized Ohio's first min-strel show troupe?

A. Daniel Decatur Emmett.

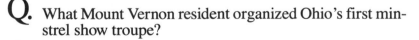

Q. What noted architect/builder lived at Painesville from 1811 to 1847?

A. Jonathan Goldsmith.

Q. What is the oldest continuously published newspaper west of the Alleghenies?

A. The Chillicothe *Gazette* (since 1800).

Q. The Toledo Museum of Art contains what concert hall that is home to the Toledo Symphony?

A. The Peristyle Concert Hall.

Q. What young Ohio writer penned *The Life of Abraham Lincoln,* which resulted in the president naming him U.S. consul to Venice?

A. William Dean Howells.

Q. What Dayton painter was well known during the 1840s and 1850s for his panoramic works based on religious themes?

A. John Insco Williams.

Q. Where is the Great Lakes Theater Festival held?

A. Playhouse Square Center, Cleveland.

Q. What Ohioan serving as a newspaper war correspondent in the 1870s earned the title of "liberator of Bulgaria"?

A. Januarius Aloysius MacGahan.

Q. Who painted the two action-packed prizefighter canvases *Both Members of This Club* and *Stag at Sharkey's?*

A. George Wesley Bellows.

Q. What comic book superhero was created in Cleveland?

A. Superman.

Q. Who in 1854 founded the Ladies Gallery of Fine Arts in Cincinnati?

A. Sarah Worthington King Peter.

Q. What "nature novel" by Allan W. Eckert told of the decline of a species of now extinct bird?

A. *The Great Auk*.

Q. The song "My Darling Nellie Gray" was written by what Westerville native?

A. Benjamin Russell Hanby.

Q. What Ohio sculptor created the pediment group for the New York Stock Exchange Building?

A. John Quincy Adams Ward.

Q. Ohio writers Jerome K. Lawrence and Robert E. Lee teamed to write what 1955 play depicting the famous Scopes trial?

A. *Inherit the Wind*.

Q. What Martins Ferry-born musician was Louis Armstrong's last regular clarinetist?

A. Joe Murany.

Q. What Ohio university features the Ohio Light Opera?

A. College of Wooster.

Q. Grounded in the school of impressionism, what Cincinnati-born painter created such works as *Waterfall, Normandy River, Springtime?*

A. John Twachtman.

Q. What noted Ohio educator was state director of the Ohio Federal Writers Project, *The Ohio Guide,* in 1940?

A. Harlan Hatcher.

Q. The 1926 structure that is now the home of the Martin Luther King Cultural Arts Center in Columbus was designed by what black architect?

A. Samuel Plato.

Q. What do the murals in the Ohio State Library depict?

A. The evolution of the printed book.

Q. What Ohio-born writer of adult humor also penned the children's books *The 13 Clocks* (1950) and *The Wonderful O* (1957)?

A. James Thurber.

Q. What great nineteenth-century American composer first was influenced by black folk music along the wharves of Cincinnati?

A. Stephen Collins Foster.

Q. Benjamin Lundy published what antislavery work in 1821 at Mount Pleasant?

A. *Genius of Universal Emancipation.*

Q. What was the first performance to inaugurate the Columbus Comstock Theater in 1855?

A. *Il Trovatore* (an opera by Verdi).

Q. Cartographer and painter Frederick Dellenbaugh, whose art chronicled many famous expeditions, was born in what Ohio community?

A. McConnelsville.

Q. What Cleveland-born musician played lead trombone on such albums as Count Basie's *Have a Nice Day* and Teresa Brewer's *Songs of Bessie Smith*?

A. Mel Wanzo.

Q. In what city did Langston Hughes, author during the 1920s Harlem Renaissance, live during his youth?

A. Cleveland.

Q. Ohio painter Alexander Wyant, who created *Adirondack Brook,* was born in what Tuscarawas County community in 1836?

A. Port Washington.

Q. What theater that opened in Cincinnati in 1859 was billed as "the grandest in the United States"?

A. Pike's Opera House.

Q. What noted architect designed Adena, the home near Chillicothe of Thomas Worthington, sixth governor of Ohio?

A. Benjamin Latrobe.

——◆——

Q. What large abstract sculpture by David Black adorns the campus of Ohio State University in Columbus?

A. *Breaker*.

——◆——

Q. When performed in Cincinnati in 1801, what work became the first theatrical presentation to play in Ohio?

A. *The Poor Soldier* (by O'Keefe).

——◆——

Q. What Middletown-born jazz pianist composed "Blue Notes on the Black and White Keys"?

A. Dave Burrell.

——◆——

Q. Ohio painter Godfrey Frankenstein created a portrait of what U.S. president?

A. John Quincy Adams.

——◆——

Q. What Warren native wrote the 1941 Pulitzer Prize-winning biography of Harriet Beecher Stowe, *Crusader in Crinoline?*

A. (Robert) Forrest Wilson.

——◆——

Q. What Painesville newspaper editor in 1834 published the first anti-Mormon book, *History of Mormonism?*

A. E. D. Howe.

Q. What Cincinnati-born pianist was Dizzy Gillespie's musical director from 1968 to 1973?

A. Mike Longo.

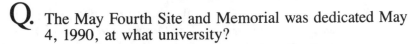

Q. The May Fourth Site and Memorial was dedicated May 4, 1990, at what university?

A. Kent State, in memory of the tragic 1970 Vietnam War protest.

Q. For what play did Steubenville native Tad Mosel receive a Pulitzer Prize in 1961?

A. *All the Way Home.*

Q. Sculptor Gutzon Borglum of Mount Rushmore fame created what work on display at Marietta?

A. Muskingum Park's *Monument to the Pioneers*.

Q. What Shakespearean actress spent part of her early childhood in Portsmouth?

A. Julia Marlowe (Fannie Brough).

Q. What Ohio-born musician became the director of the Davey Moore Arts Cultural Center in Springfield?

A. Johnny Lytle.

Q. *The Ohio Harmonist* (1847) was but one of several song books compiled and published by what popular Deersville songmaster?

A. Alexander Auld.

Q. In what Ohio city did Lafcadio Hearn gain notoriety as a reporter?

A. Cincinnati.

———◆———

Q. What nineteenth-century Ohio sculptor created such noted works as *Evangeline, Eve Disconsolate,* and *Greek Slave* after relocation in Florence, Italy?

A. Hiram Powers.

———◆———

Q. The gifted artist brothers John Quincy Adams Ward and Edgar Melville Ward were born in what community?

A. Urbana.

———◆———

Q. What nationally famous, Louisville-born keyboard player studied piano and organ at Mount Union College and received a B.S. from the Cincinnati Conservatory of Music?

A. Pat Rebillot.

———◆———

Q. What Akron native founded the American Repertory Theatre?

A. Cheryl Crawford.

———◆———

Q. How did critics of Cincinnati-born painter Robert Henri label his style of painting?

A. The Ashcan School.

———◆———

Q. The Cleveland Conservatory of Music was founded in what year?

A. 1881.

SPORTS & LEISURE

C H A P T E R   F I V E

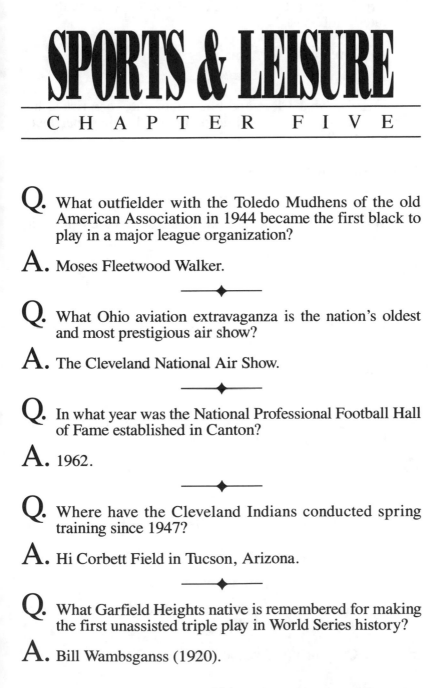

Q. What outfielder with the Toledo Mudhens of the old American Association in 1944 became the first black to play in a major league organization?

A. Moses Fleetwood Walker.

———◆———

Q. What Ohio aviation extravaganza is the nation's oldest and most prestigious air show?

A. The Cleveland National Air Show.

———◆———

Q. In what year was the National Professional Football Hall of Fame established in Canton?

A. 1962.

———◆———

Q. Where have the Cleveland Indians conducted spring training since 1947?

A. Hi Corbett Field in Tucson, Arizona.

———◆———

Q. What Garfield Heights native is remembered for making the first unassisted triple play in World Series history?

A. Bill Wambsganss (1920).

Q. What Portsmouth-born outfielder almost died with an allergic reaction to nuts in a cake sent by a fan to the Pirates' clubhouse?

A. Al Oliver.

Q. In 1920 what Cleveland-born major leaguer risked his career to save fifteen children from a blazing apartment building?

A. Dode Paskert.

Q. Where are mule-drawn canal boat rides on the Ohio-Erie Canal available?

A. Tuscarawas and Canal Fulton.

Q. In what years were the Cincinnati Bengals the American Football Conference champions?

A. 1982 and 1988.

Q. What Cincinnati pitcher tops the team's all-time National League victory list with 179 wins?

A. Eppa Rixey.

Q. What amusement park is at Geneva-on-the-Lake?

A. Erieview Amusement Park.

Q. Who is the only player in major league history to have died from a pitched ball?

A. Ray Chapman (Cleveland Indians, 1920).

Q. Situated near Mansfield, what is the name of Ohio's first ski resort?

A. Snow Trails.

———◆———

Q. What former Ohio State starting flanker was chosen as a Rhodes Scholar in 1985?

A. Mike Lanese.

———◆———

Q. In 1889 the Cleveland ball club was given what nickname because of its tall, skinny players?

A. Spiders.

———◆———

Q. What Ohio State center scored 49 points in one game, setting a school basketball record in 1964?

A. Gary Bradds.

———◆———

Q. Who became the first member of the Cincinnati Reds' Walk of Fame?

A. Johnny Bench.

———◆———

Q. The Bowling Green State University Falcons display what colors?

A. Brown and orange.

———◆———

Q. Major league catcher Johnny Roseboro was born in what city?

A. Ashland.

Q. Golf great Jack Nicklaus is native to what city?

A. Columbus.

Q. Thomas C. Eakin founded what state sports museum, the only state museum of its kind in the nation?

A. The Ohio Baseball Hall of Fame.

Q. A 953-foot course is the object of attention at what annual Akron youth event?

A. The All-American Soap Box Derby.

Q. *Sporting News* named what Portsmouth-born catcher minor leagues' Manager of the Year in 1971?

A. Del Rice.

Q. What community hosts the annual Lorain County Fair each August?

A. Wellington.

Q. At the conclusion of the 1986 season, what Buckeye ranked as the school's career leader in tackles with 572?

A. Marcus Marek.

Q. For what Ohio team did Cy Young pitch prior to coming to the Cleveland Indians in 1909?

A. Cleveland Nationals (1890–1898).

Q. Where did the Cincinnati Reds play home games prior to the opening of Riverfront Stadium?

A. Crosley Field.

Q. What Loudonville canoe livery is the oldest firm of its type in the state?

A. Mohican Canoe Livery.

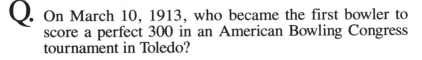

Q. How many home runs did Cleveland Indian star Wes Ferrell hit in 1931, setting a standing major league record for a pitcher?

A. Nine.

Q. In what year did the Cleveland Browns join the National Football League?

A. 1950.

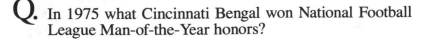

Q. On March 10, 1913, who became the first bowler to score a perfect 300 in an American Bowling Congress tournament in Toledo?

A. William Knox.

Q. Cincinnati-born outfielder Jim Wynn was given what nickname?

A. Toy Cannon.

Q. In 1975 what Cincinnati Bengal won National Football League Man-of-the-Year honors?

A. Ken Anderson.

Q. How many gold medals did Ohio-educated Jesse Owens receive at the 1936 Olympics in Berlin?

A. Four.

———◆———

Q. What former Ohio State Buckeye is college football's only two-time Heisman Trophy winner?

A. Archie Griffin.

———◆———

Q. What Cincinnati Reds player led the National League in pinch-hits in 1986?

A. Kal Daniels.

———◆———

Q. What Cleveland native is remembered as one of the first pitchers to throw a slider?

A. George ("Bull") Uhle.

———◆———

Q. What U.S. president started the baseball opening day tradition of throwing out the first ball?

A. Ohioan William Howard Taft.

———◆———

Q. What two Buckeyes received All-America first team basketball honors in 1962?

A. John Havlicek and Jerry Lucas.

———◆———

Q. What renowned American League shortstop managed the Cleveland Indians in 1941 and was vice president/ general manager 1942–46?

A. Roger Peckinpaugh.

Q. Who kicked Ohio State's longest field goal in the final game of the 1986 season?

A. Tom Skladany (59 yards at Illinois, November 8).

———◆———

Q. In 1971 what Crestline native set a new American League record of 81 career pinch-hits?

A. Gates Brown.

———◆———

Q. In honor of what American Indian, the first to play in the major leagues, were the Cleveland Indians named?

A. Luis Francis Sockalexis.

———◆———

Q. What is Cleveland's National Basketball Association team?

A. The Cavaliers.

———◆———

Q. Kent State University home football games are played where?

A. Dix Stadium.

———◆———

Q. What Cincinnati native received the Hickok Award in 1975 as the top professional athlete of the year?

A. Pete Rose.

———◆———

Q. For what two major league teams did Ohioan Woody English play?

A. Chicago Cubs and Brooklyn Dodgers.

Q. What Chardon attraction offers a large water theme park and more than 400 campsites?

A. Pioneer Waterland Park and Campground.

Q. The annual National Jigsaw Puzzle Championship is held in what city?

A. Athens.

Q. What Ohio State linebacker was named Top Defensive Player in the 1986 Cotton Bowl?

A. Chris Spielman.

Q. What Cincinnati Red ranks as the second home run leader (following Johnny Bench) in Riverfront Stadium with 128?

A. George Foster.

Q. What nickname belongs to the University of Dayton?

A. The Flyers.

Q. Toledo native Dick Drago played for what team in the 1975 World Series?

A. Boston Red Sox.

Q. What ski resort near Bellefontaine features a 1,400-foot Alpine slide?

A. Mad River Mountain Ski Resort.

Q. In what Brown County village was major league pitcher Slim Sallee born and raised?

A. Higgensport.

Q. What four Cincinnati Bengals were selected to play in the 1986 Pro Bowl?

A. Anthony Munoz, James Brooks, Boomer Esiason, and Max Montoya.

Q. In 1869 what Cincinnati team was the first in professional baseball history to pay a regular salary?

A. The Red Stockings.

Q. What Ohio-born hurler pitched for the Minnesota Twins in the 1987 World Series?

A. Joe Niekro.

Q. In Big Ten basketball, what was the final regular season conference standing for Ohio State in 1990–91?

A. First.

Q. What football team comprised of Jim Thorpe and other Indian athletes played out of La Rue?

A. The Oorang Indians.

Q. At a single track meet Jesse Owens set three world records and tied a fourth while attending what Ohio university?

A. Ohio State University.

Q. Whom did Ohio State defeat, 13–3, on February 16, 1898, in its first basketball game?

A. North High School.

Q. What Cleveland Indian was the only player to play all 162 games in a season without making an error?

A. Rocky Colavito.

Q. Al Rosen hit how many home runs for Cleveland during the 1953 season?

A. Forty-three.

Q. What Outland Trophy recipient was the first round draft choice of the Cincinnati Bengals in 1987?

A. Jason Buck.

Q. The legendary Cy Young was a native of what community?

A. Gilmore.

Q. In 1978 who became the first Reds shortstop in sixty-five years to top the .300 mark?

A. Dave Concepcion.

Q. At what age did Tribesman Satchel Paige pitch his first complete major league game?

A. Forty-two.

Q. On August 7, 1932, what major leaguer hit the first home run at Cleveland Stadium?

A. Indian infielder Johnny Burnett.

———◆———

Q. What school won the 1985–86 men's basketball championship in the Ohio Athletic Conference?

A. Otterbein College.

———◆———

Q. Under what manager did the Cincinnati Reds go to the World Series four times in the 1970s?

A. "Sparky" Anderson.

———◆———

Q. What social organization for men over age seventy was founded by Dr. Leroy Pence at Lima in 1931?

A. The Borrowed Time Club.

———◆———

Q. In how many Rose Bowl games did Buckeye Archie Griffin participate?

A. Four.

———◆———

Q. The uniforms of what former Cleveland Indians have been retired?

A. Earl Averill (number 3), Lou Boudreau (number 5), and Bob Feller (number 19).

———◆———

Q. What Ney native was the only pitcher in major league history to win twenty games for a club that lost one hundred games during the same season?

A. Ned Garver (1951, St. Louis Browns).

Q. What Ravenna-based firm offers scenic hot air balloon flights over northern Ohio?

A. Roaring Silence Balloon Port.

Q. How many home runs were hit by Cleveland in the record-setting 1966 game against the Detroit Tigers?

A. Seven.

Q. Who was named Coach of the Year on the World Almanac All-American basketball team in 1991?

A. Randy Ayers, Ohio State.

Q. What Ohio State football coach played the "three yards and a cloud of dust" system?

A. Woody Hayes.

Q. What is Ohio's largest ski area?

A. Brandywine Ski Center.

Q. What Hamilton-born pitcher was the youngest player ever to participate in a major league game?

A. Joe Nuxhall (age fifteen).

Q. What Cincinnati Reds hurler pitched a no-hitter against St. Louis on June 16, 1978?

A. Tom Seaver.

Q. What Tribesman was the first black pitcher to pitch in a World Series game?

A. Satchel Paige (game 5, 1948).

Q. Ohio State defeated what opponent, 28–12, in the 1987 Cotton Bowl?

A. Texas A&M.

Q. Where is the National Football Foundation's College Football Hall of Fame?

A. Kings Island.

Q. Akron hosts what national bowling event each April?

A. The Firestone Tournament of Bowling Champions.

Q. In what community is Roche de Boeuf Day held in honor of the Rock of the Buffalo in the Maumee River?

A. Waterville.

Q. The Cleveland Indians closed the 1991 season with what batting average?

A. .254.

Q. What Brownhelm-born National League manager led the Brooklyn Dodgers to pennants in 1947 and 1949?

A. Burt Shotton.

Q. What Cleveland Indian was the first pitcher to hit a home run in a World Series game?

A. Jim Bagby (1920).

Q. Who designed the Muirfield Country Club golf course in Columbus?

A. Jack Nicklaus.

Q. What Ohio State basketball player holds the school's record for most rebounds in one season?

A. Jerry Lucas (499 in 1962).

Q. By what name is the Cincinnati Bengals' mascot affectionately called?

A. Benzoo.

Q. What was the score of the 1990 World Series?

A. Cincinnati 4, Oakland 0.

Q. What Baseball Hall of Fame member born in Hoaglands began his catching career with the Mohawk Browns in Cincinnati?

A. Buck Ewing.

Q. Where may the state's "sweetest" celebration, the Ohio Honey Festival, be enjoyed each September?

A. Lebanon.

Q. Ohio's largest fashion show takes place during what spectacular event?

A. The Pro Football Hall of Fame Festival.

Q. What Columbus Clippers moundsman holds the team record for the longest winning streak?

A. Dave Wehrmeister (nine in 1981).

Q. The Cincinnati Reds have retired the uniform numbers of what players?

A. Fred Hutchinson (number 1) and Johnny Bench (number 5).

Q. With 2,096 points, what Ohio State forward became the school's career scoring leader?

A. Dennis Hopson.

Q. Shortstop Neal Ball was playing for what team when he made the first recorded unassisted triple play in modern major league history?

A. Cleveland Indians (1909).

Q. Coach Earle Bruce led how many Buckeye teams to Big Ten championships?

A. Four.

Q. In 1975 what Cleveland Indian manager became the first black to hold that position in the major leagues?

A. Frank Robinson.

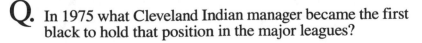

Q. What Marietta native played nineteen years in the major leagues, then umpired for the National League in 1904–05?

A. Charles ("Chief") Zimmer.

Q. How many touchdowns did Buckeye Art Schlichter throw in his Ohio State career?

A. Eighty-five.

Q. What was the score of the Liberty Bowl at Memphis in 1990?

A. Air Force 23, Ohio State 11.

Q. Snow machines at Mad River Mountain Ski Area can produce how many tons of snow per minute?

A. Five.

Q. What Columbus-born major league catcher succeeded Bill McKechnie as manager of the Cincinnati Reds?

A. Hank Gowdy.

Q. Corcoran Field serves as the stadium for what Ohio university?

A. Xavier.

Q. Whom did Jack Dempsey defeat in Toledo on July 4, 1919, to win the heavyweight championship of the world?

A. Jess Willard.

Q. How many Ohio State coaches are members of the National Football Hall of Fame?

A. Five (Howard Jones, Dr. John W. Wilee, Francis A. Schmidt, Ernest R. Godfrey, and Woody Hayes).

———◆———

Q. What Cincinnati-born member of the Baseball Hall of Fame is credited with directing the New York Yankees to their first series of pennants and world championships?

A. Miller Huggins.

———◆———

Q. In 1984 what association was formed to aid in the activities of Cleveland Browns fan clubs?

A. Browns Backers.

———◆———

Q. What Columbus Clipper set the all-time high batting average at .335?

A. Scott Bradley (1984).

———◆———

Q. In 1987 what Ohioan became the only person in the state's history to have a day proclaimed in his honor by at least one village or city in every county?

A. Thomas C. Eakin.

———◆———

Q. Former Ohio State Buckeye Todd Bell joined what NFL team following his college career?

A. Chicago Bears.

———◆———

Q. Both the Charles D. Hill Trot Championship and the Wayne ("Curly") Smart Pace Championship are held in what city?

A. Columbus.

Q. What Ohio State basketball guard scored more points (2,958) than any other male player in the state's high school history?

A. Jay Burson (New Concord).

———◆———

Q. With seventy-three solos and forty assists, what Cincinnati Bengal was the leading team tackler in 1986?

A. Tim Krumrie.

———◆———

Q. Woodsfield native Sad Sam Jones pitched how many consecutive years for the American League?

A. Twenty-two.

———◆———

Q. Who was the second Ohio State player to receive the Heisman Trophy?

A. Vic Janowicz, 1950.

———◆———

Q. By what nickname is Muskingum College known?

A. Fighting Muskies.

———◆———

Q. Where is the Trapshooting Hall of Fame and Museum?

A. Vandalia.

———◆———

Q. What Reds team member became the oldest player to hit a grand slam in the majors one day before his forty-third birthday?

A. Tony Perez (1985).

Q. What Ohio city has a rugby football club?

A. Cleveland.

———◆———

Q. Cleveland native Mike Easler played in the 1979 World Series for what club?

A. Pittsburgh Pirates.

———◆———

Q. The Cleveland Browns have retired the jerseys of what five players?

A. Otto Graham (number 14), Jim Brown (number 32), Ernie Davis (number 45), Don Fleming (number 46), and Lou Groza (number 76).

———◆———

Q. What Lorain County-born pitcher is best remembered for his accusation that Ty Cobb and Tris Speaker had bet on a 1919 Detroit Tigers vs. Cleveland Indians game?

A. Dutch Leonard.

———◆———

Q. Setting a modern National League record in 1978, Pete Rose established a hitting streak in how many consecutive games?

A. Forty-four.

———◆———

Q. What Ohio State Buckeye holds the individual record for most consecutive extra points made?

A. Vlade Janakievski (47: 44 in 1977; 3 in 1978).

———◆———

Q. What classic fall harness race is held at Delaware?

A. The Little Brown Jug.

Q. Where is the USGA Women's Open and the NEC World Series of Golf held?

A. The Firestone Country Club in Akron.

Q. At age forty-six, what Blaine native became the oldest major league pitcher to hurl a shutout on October 6, 1985?

A. Phil Niekro.

Q. In what Ohio community was major league pitcher Grant Jackson born?

A. Fostoria.

Q. Who was the youngest player ever to play for the Cleveland Indians?

A. Bob Feller (seventeen years of age, 1936).

Q. Who was the first Ohio State recipient of the Heisman Trophy?

A. Les Horvath (1944).

Q. Where is the grueling Escort 24 Hours at the Mid-Ohio stock car race held?

A. Mid-Ohio Sports Car Course, Lexington.

Q. What trap shooting accessory was patented by George Ligowsky of Cincinnati on September 7, 1880?

A. Clay pigeon target.

Q. First held in 1823, what is the oldest county fair in Ohio?

A. The Great Geauga County Fair, Burton.

Q. In 1975 whom did Cleveland Indian fans select as the most memorable Tribesman?

A. Rocky Colavito.

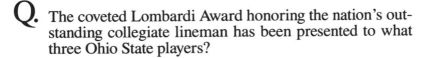

Q. What Cincinnati Red has recorded twenty or more home runs and eighty or more stolen bases in the same season?

A. Eric Davis.

Q. The coveted Lombardi Award honoring the nation's outstanding collegiate lineman has been presented to what three Ohio State players?

A. Jim Stillwagon (1970), John Hicks (1973), and Chris Spielman (1987).

Q. What Wayne-born pitcher led the American League in shutouts (eleven) in 1964 and went on to receive the Cy Young Award that same year?

A. Dean Chance.

Q. What Ohio State athlete received the Heisman Trophy in 1955?

A. Howard ("Hopalong") Cassady.

Q. Syracuse native Rollie Hemsley played with what major league pennant winner during his nineteen-year career?

A. Chicago Cubs.

Q. Noted for its German sausage, what town holds a Bratwurst Festival each August?

A. Bucyrus.

Q. What Niles-born Boston Red Sox first baseman made an unforgettable unassisted triple play against Cleveland in 1923?

A. George Burns.

Q. In what year did Ohio State win its first Big Ten Basketball Championship?

A. 1925.

Q. What Cincinnati-born veteran followed his thirteen-year major league career by coaching at Yale University for more than twenty years?

A. Ethan Allen.

Q. Cleveland Browns nose tackle Bob Golic attended what Cleveland high school?

A. St. Joseph's.

Q. On what 1846 sternwheeler steamboat may one cruise the Maumee River at Toledo?

A. The *Shawnee Princess*.

Q. Cincinnati's Johnny Bench set what club career record for home runs?

A. 389.

Q. In what Ohio stadium were played the only two major league games in which no assists were made?

A. Cleveland Stadium (1943 and 1945).

———◆———

Q. Track star Edwin Moses was born in what Ohio city?

A. Dayton.

———◆———

Q. What great Ohio-born relief pitcher was known for wearing a handlebar mustache?

A. Rollie Fingers.

———◆———

Q. The sport of *steinstossen,* popular at the Ohio Swiss Festival in Sugarcreek, requires what athletic prowess?

A. Hurling a 138-pound stone.

———◆———

Q. Who took ownership of the Cleveland Browns in March of 1961?

A. Arthur B. Modell.

———◆———

Q. What semiprofessional basketball team plays in Youngstown?

A. The Youngstown Pride.

———◆———

Q. In what year was Ohio first represented in a World Series contest?

A. 1919 (Cincinnati Reds vs. Chicago White Sox).

Q. What Indians moundsman pitched the first American League night no-hitter?

A. Bob Lemon (June 30, 1948).

———◆———

Q. In 1914 what famous race car driver competed at Columbus against daredevil pilot Lincoln Beachey?

A. Barney Oldfield.

———◆———

Q. What Tribesman was the first player/manager in the majors to win a pennant?

A. Lou Boudreau.

———◆———

Q. The first national skeet tournament was held August 31, 1935, in what Ohio community?

A. Solon.

———◆———

Q. Toledo native George Mullin pitched in the 1907, 1908, and 1909 World Series for what American League team?

A. Detroit Tigers.

———◆———

Q. By the end of the 1986 season, what Cleveland Browns defensive end led the club with sixty-four consecutive games started?

A. Reggie Camp.

———◆———

Q. What Ohio State All-America end coached the Buckeyes from 1947–50?

A. Wesley E. Fesler.

Q. At the National Outdoor Rifle and Pistol Championships in 1991, who won competitions in Smallbore Rifle Prone and Civilian Smallbore Rifle Prone?

A. Ronald O. West of Zanesville.

Q. Who was selected the outstanding Cincinnati Reds pitcher of the year in 1986?

A. John Franco.

Q. What high-speed racing event is held each spring on the Maumee River in downtown Toledo?

A. The Toledo International Grand Prix Hydroplane Races.

Q. Milan is known for what celebration featuring such treats as muskmelon ice cream and watermelon sherbet?

A. The Melon Festival.

Q. What three Indians pitchers have each struck out four men in one inning?

A. Guy Morton (1916), Lee Stange (1964), and Mike Paxton (1978).

Q. In 1970 what Akron-born Yankee catcher was named Rookie of the Year in the American League?

A. Thurman Munson.

Q. During what years did Woody Hayes coach at Ohio State?

A. 1951–78.

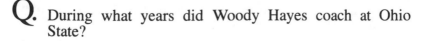

Q. Situated at Kings Island, what is the world's fastest and longest roller coaster?

A. The Beast.

———◆———

Q. What players were Ohio State's top three ground gainers during the 1986 season?

A. Vince Workman, Jaymes Bryant, and George Cooper.

———◆———

Q. In 1982 what pitcher set the Cincinnati Reds individual season strike-out record with 274?

A. Mario Soto.

———◆———

Q. What two football teams played in the October 17, 1971, game that witnessed the largest crowd ever (60,284) for a sporting event at Riverfront Stadium?

A. Cincinnati Bengals and Cleveland Browns.

———◆———

Q. What Cleveland native pitched in the 1979 World Series for the Baltimore Orioles?

A. Steve Stone.

———◆———

Q. Where are the annual National Tractor Pulling Championships held?

A. Wood County Fairgrounds, Bowling Green.

———◆———

Q. What is the name of the Thoroughbred track at North Randall?

A. Thistledown Racing Club.

Q. In what year did the Cleveland Indians first use the "Chief Wahoo" logo?

A. 1947 (on the jersey sleeve).

Q. Against what team in 1988 did Cincinnati Red Tom Browning pitch a perfect major league game for a score of 1–0?

A. Los Angeles Dodgers.

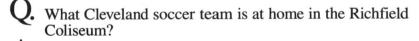

Q. What outstanding win/loss record was established by pitcher Cy Young?

A. 511 wins/313 losses.

Q. Who in 1927 led the Toledo Mudhens to their first championship in the American Association?

A. Casey Stengel.

Q. What Cleveland soccer team is at home in the Richfield Coliseum?

A. Cleveland Force.

Q. The Baseball Writers' Association of America named what Dayton-born Cleveland Indian American League Rookie of the Year in 1971?

A. Chris Chambliss.

Q. What championship fight opened the Cleveland Stadium on July 3, 1931?

A. The Schmeling–Stribling heavyweight match.

Q. Ohio State plays all home basketball games in what arena?

A. St. John Arena.

Q. Cleveland-born Ed Delahanty was one of how many brothers to play major league baseball?

A. Five.

Q. What Cincinnati-born pitcher formed a famous clown baseball act with fellow Washington Senator Al Schacht?

A. Nick Altrock.

Q. Situated at North Field, what is the Midwest's largest water theme park?

A. Brandywine's Dover Lake Park.

Q. Cincinnati's Dave Parker was traded to what major league franchise in 1987?

A. Oakland A's.

Q. The Cuyahoga Valley National Recreation Area along the Cuyahoga River between Cleveland and Akron contains how many acres?

A. 33,000.

Q. In November 1987 what Ohio native became manager of the Chicago Cubs?

A. Don Zimmer.

Q. In 1983 what Cleveland Browns kicker won the NFL kicking title by making twenty-one of twenty-four field goal attempts?

A. Matt Bahr.

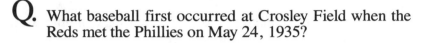

Q. What baseball first occurred at Crosley Field when the Reds met the Phillies on May 24, 1935?

A. The first night game by major league teams.

Q. Hall of Fame member Rube Marquard enjoyed eighteen years in the major league at what position?

A. Pitcher.

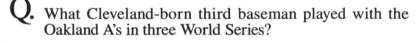

Q. Rajahland recreation park, complete with swimming, sports, and a waterslide, is in what Ohio community?

A. Amherst.

Q. What Cleveland-born third baseman played with the Oakland A's in three World Series?

A. Sal Bando.

Q. What Cincinnati Reds infielder was the first baseball player twice named Most Valuable Player of the Big Ten Conference?

A. Barry Larkin.

Q. Darby Downs, which features both Thoroughbred and quarterhorse racing, is situated where?

A. Grove City.

Q. What three-time Ohio State All-American is credited with first arousing the excitement of Columbus residents about Buckeye football?

A. Charles ("Chick") Harley.

Q. Who won the Cincinnati Reds first batting championship in 1905 with a .377 hitting mark?

A. Cy Seymour.

Q. Champion drag racing is featured at what Hebron strip?

A. National Trail Raceway.

Q. Which Cleveland catcher caught 152 out of 154 games in 1949?

A. Jim Hegan.

Q. What vintage-1918 train runs excursions between Independence and Akron?

A. Cuyahoga Valley Line Steam Railroad.

Q. Each Memorial Day weekend the Rock Rhythm 'n' Blues Festival takes place in what city?

A. Toledo.

Q. Former Buckeye Archie Griffin played eight years for what National Football League team?

A. Cincinnati Bengals.

Q. What Toledoan inducted into the Cooperstown Hall of Fame in 1945 introduced shin guards for catchers?

A. Roger Bresnahan.

Q. At what annual Rio Grande event do contestants nudge a fowl into flight?

A. International Chicken Flying Meet (at Bob Evans Farm).

Q. Cincinnati-born outfielder Bob Nieman participated in the 1962 World Series for what National League team?

A. San Francisco Giants.

Q. In what year did the Ohio State Buckeyes first play football in Ohio Stadium?

A. 1922.

Q. What Cleveland Indian was the first black player to bat in an American League game?

A. Larry Doby.

Q. Cedar Point at Sandusky features what exciting ride with cars suspended below a track to create the sensation of free flight?

A. The Iron Dragon.

Q. Cincinnati-born outfielder Garry Maddox played for what National League team in 1980 and 1983?

A. Philadelphia Phillies.

Q. What International Hockey League team is based in Toledo?

A. The Goaldiggers Hockey Club.

Q. For what major league team did Jim and Gaylord Perry play when they set the American League record for most wins by brothers pitching on the same team?

A. Cleveland Indians (1974–75).

Q. What Cleveland Browns quarterback spent the entire 1986 season on the bench because of an injury?

A. Gary Danielson.

Q. How many times does the twelve-story steel coaster, the Vortex, at Kings Island turn the ride upside down?

A. Six times.

Q. What Portsmouth native is credited with establishing the minor league farm system?

A. Branch Rickey.

Q. Paul Brown, Weeb Ewbank, and Ara Parseghian are part of what university's gridiron history?

A. Miami University, Oxford.

Q. What Xenia sports facility provides participants with "high" adventure?

A. The Greene County Skydiving Center.

Q. What term referred to the powerful Cincinnati Reds during the 1970s?

A. "The Big Red Machine."

————◆————

Q. Cincinnati-born infielder Don Zimmer participated in the 1955 and 1959 World Series for what teams?

A. Brooklyn Dodgers and Los Angeles Dodgers.

————◆————

Q. In what year did the Columbus Clippers, the New York Yankees' AAA minor league affiliate, join the International League?

A. 1977.

————◆————

Q. From 1903 through 1991, in how many World Series contests have the Cleveland Indians and Cincinnati Reds participated?

A. Twelve.

————◆————

Q. What West Salem drag strip features national championship racing?

A. Drag Way 42.

————◆————

Q. What Cincinnati Reds hurler is the only major league pitcher to record back-to-back no-hitters?

A. Johnny Vander Meer (1938).

————◆————

Q. In 1920 what Cleveland Indian hit the first World Series grand slam?

A. Elmer Smith.

Q. What playing position was held by Bedford native Elmer Flick during his thirteen years in the major leagues?

A. Outfielder.

Q. Pitcher Leon Kessling ("Red") Ames of Warren played in the 1905, 1911, and 1912 World Series for what ball club?

A. New York Giants.

Q. What is one of the few remaining chautauguas in the country, serving as a center for recreation, entertainment, education, and culture?

A. Lakeside on Marblehead Peninsula.

Q. Where do the Toledo Mudhens play their home games?

A. Lucas County Stadium.

Q. Ohioan Cy Young set the existing record for how many complete games pitched?

A. 751.

Q. Springfield is the site of what bike racing course?

A. Lagonda BMX Race Park.

Q. In 1968 what Columbus-born outfielder hit ten home runs in twenty at bats over a span of six games?

A. Frank Howard.

Q. Because of his speech and hearing difficulties, what Houcktown-born major leaguer is credited with the system umpires use of raising the hand to call strikes?

A. William E. ("Dummy") Hoy.

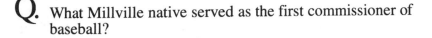

Q. Clayton-born pitcher Jesse Haines was elected to the Baseball Hall of Fame for his 210–158 record for what ball club?

A. St. Louis Cardinals (1920–37).

Q. Where was powerful major league veteran Bob Fothergill born?

A. Massillon.

Q. What Millville native served as the first commissioner of baseball?

A. Kenesaw Mountain Landis.

Q. What track is the home of the International Hot Rod Association's Winston World Nationals?

A. Norwalk Raceway Park.

Q. What three Cleveland Indians pitchers each hit .300 and won twenty games in a season?

A. George Uhle (1923), Joe Shaute (1924), and Wes Ferrell (1931).

Q. What Medway native pitched a twelve-inning, no-hit ball game for the Pittsburgh Pirates, only to lose to the Milwaukee Braves in the thirteenth inning, 1–0?

A. Harvey Haddix.

Q. What Cincinnati Reds outfielder claimed Most Valuable Player honors in 1984, 1985, and 1986?

A. Dave Parker.

Q. As of 1991, how many times has Cincinnati won the World Series?

A. Five (1919, 1940, 1975, 1976, 1990).

Q. St. Wendelin-born outfielder Wally Post played in the 1961 World Series for what club?

A. Cincinnati Reds.

Q. What Columbus-born catcher, who led the National League in most games caught, fielding, most putouts, most assists, and most total chances, also graduated from Ohio State in the same year?

A. Johnny Edwards.

Q. At Ravenna on October 18, 1930, what jockey was the first ever to win seven races in one day?

A. Joseph Sylvester.

Q. What Manchester-born 1939 Hall of Famer set the major league record for most lifetime assists with 1,554?

A. George Sisler.

Q. What major leaguer hit the first home run at Riverfront Stadium on June 30, 1970?

A. Hank Aaron.

SCIENCE & NATURE

C H A P T E R   S I X

Q. What flower was designated the official Ohio state flower in 1904?

A. The scarlet carnation.

———◆———

Q. Between 1934 and 1939, radio station WLW in Cincinnati was given an experimental license by the federal government to operate with what amount of power?

A. 500,000 watts.

———◆———

Q. Johnny Appleseed believed his efforts to establish apple orchards would help pioneer families avoid what malady?

A. Scurvy.

———◆———

Q. What fossil remains were unearthed by a Johnstown resident while working in his garden in August of 1926?

A. A mastodon skeleton.

———◆———

Q. What mound was the first recognized remains of the Adena Indian culture?

A. Story Mound State Memorial, Chillicothe.

Q. What is the name of Toledo's botanical gardens?

A. Crosby Gardens.

————◆————

Q. Where in Ohio may one go on a drive-through safari complete with lions, giraffe, zebra, and elephants?

A. African Lion Safari, Port Clinton.

————◆————

Q. What city has been called the Cardinal Capital?

A. Cincinnati.

————◆————

Q. The 125-acre Cleveland Metroparks Zoo is home to how many animals?

A. Over 1,300.

————◆————

Q. What are the two leading rubber products produced in Akron?

A. Inner tubes and tires.

————◆————

Q. What is Ohio's national rank in number of wineries?

A. Third (sixth in overall production).

————◆————

Q. How many burial mounds are included in the Mound City Group National Monument near Chillicothe?

A. Twenty-three.

Q. What is the only variety of hummingbird to be found in Ohio?

A. The ruby-throated hummingbird.

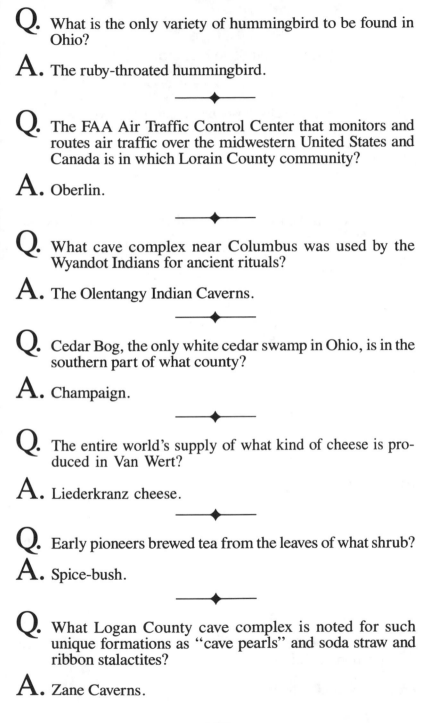

Q. The FAA Air Traffic Control Center that monitors and routes air traffic over the midwestern United States and Canada is in which Lorain County community?

A. Oberlin.

Q. What cave complex near Columbus was used by the Wyandot Indians for ancient rituals?

A. The Olentangy Indian Caverns.

Q. Cedar Bog, the only white cedar swamp in Ohio, is in the southern part of what county?

A. Champaign.

Q. The entire world's supply of what kind of cheese is produced in Van Wert?

A. Liederkranz cheese.

Q. Early pioneers brewed tea from the leaves of what shrub?
A. Spice-bush.

Q. What Logan County cave complex is noted for such unique formations as "cave pearls" and soda straw and ribbon stalactites?

A. Zane Caverns.

Q. What is the largest conical mound in Ohio?

A. Miamisburg Mound State Memorial.

Q. What town annually hosts the largest organized "birdwalk" in the nation?

A. Hinckley.

Q. Where was the first public weather service established in 1869?

A. Cincinnati.

Q. What Antwerp attraction displays over 500 mounted birds and animals?

A. Ehrhart Museum.

Q. Cleveland resident Garrett A. Morgan received $40,000 from General Electric in 1923 for what revolutionary invention?

A. An electric stop sign.

Q. In 1836 the state's first operational railroad line (from Toledo to Adrian, Michigan) used what mode of power?

A. Horses.

Q. What is the dominant rock structure underlying a large portion of Ohio?

A. Cincinnati anticline.

Q. What state forest contains Ohio's oldest pine plantation?

A. Zaleski State Forest.

———◆———

Q. What is the official Ohio state bird?

A. The cardinal.

———◆———

Q. Lucy, said to be the oldest and most complete human fossil skeleton found so far, is on display at what Ohio museum?

A. Cleveland Museum of Natural History.

———◆———

Q. What prolific Columbus-born scientist is credited with the invention of an incubator (1900) and automatic air brakes (1902)?

A. Granville T. Woods.

———◆———

Q. In what land region is the most fertile farming soil found?

A. The Till Plains.

———◆———

Q. What agency regulates the release of pollutants into the Ohio River?

A. The Ohio River Valley Water Sanitation Commission.

———◆———

Q. In 1814 Silas Thorla drilled the first oil well in America near what Nobel County community?

A. Caldwell.

Q. What insect traveled from Europe to the United States in 1910, causing great damage to Ohio corn crops?

A. Corn borer.

———◆———

Q. What Delphos farm boy turned amateur astronomer received international recognition for his discovery of various comets?

A. Leslie Peltier.

———◆———

Q. What is the length of the Great Serpent Mound in northern Adams County?

A. 1,330 feet.

———◆———

Q. In what city was the twenty-four-hour banking machine introduced?

A. Columbus.

———◆———

Q. What three varieties of poisonous snakes are found in Ohio?

A. Copperhead, cottonmouth, and rattlesnake.

———◆———

Q. Where does Ohio rank among the other states in the amount of greenhouse vegetables produced?

A. First.

———◆———

Q. What was Ohio's first mining industry?

A. Salt mining.

Q. Proctorville is the home of what variety of apple, first grown there in 1816?

A. Rome Beauty.

Q. What Ohio zoo started with a woodchuck, a golden eagle, and two badgers?

A. The Toledo Zoo.

Q. A Braille trail for the blind is a unique part of what Harrison park?

A. Miami Whitewater Forest.

Q. What percentage of the nation's building sandstone is produced in Ohio?

A. About one-third.

Q. In 1834 Felix Renick from the Chillicothe area became the first person in the nation to import what kind of European livestock?

A. Full-blooded shorthorn cattle.

Q. What Ohio-born astronaut was the first person ever to set foot on the moon?

A. Neil A. Armstrong.

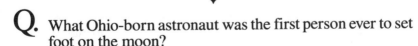

Q. High swiss cheese production in Tuscarawas County has earned it what nickname?

A. America's Little Switzerland.

Q. What much celebrated breed of hogs was developed in Warren County during the nineteenth century?

A. Poland China.

Q. What cave near West Liberty is the largest in Ohio?

A. Ohio Caverns.

Q. What is the official Ohio state tree?

A. The buckeye.

Q. Over 100 major exhibits pertaining to health may be viewed at what Cleveland attraction?

A. Cleveland Health Education Museum.

Q. What state wildlife area covers 4,672 acres in portions of Holmes and Wayne counties?

A. Killbuck Marsh Wildlife Area.

Q. The Portsmouth Area Project in Pike County, developed under the Atomic Energy Commission, produces what kind of nuclear reactor fuel?

A. Uranium–235.

Q. What makes up 95 percent of a cardinal hatchling's diet?

A. Insects.

Q. On February 23, 1886, what Oberlin resident discovered the electrolytic process for making aluminum?

A. Charles Martin Hall.

Q. How many bushels of corn were produced in Ohio in 1850?

A. Sixty million.

Q. What Canton agricultural inventor was noted for his improvement of the plow in 1836?

A. Joshua Gibbs.

Q. The original chapter of the National Polio Foundation was chartered in what Ohio community in 1938?

A. Coshocton.

Q. What Clevelander invented the arc light in 1876?

A. Charles Brush.

Q. The former home of author, farmer, and conservationist Louis Bromfield is now what state park devoted to conservation and education?

A. Malabar Farm, near Mansfield.

Q. What two types of vultures are found in Ohio?

A. Turkey and black vultures.

Q. What is Ohio's lowest recorded temperature?

A. -39° F (at Milligan, February 10, 1899).

Q. How does the average wind velocity of Cleveland compare with that of Chicago, the "Windy City"?

A. Cleveland: 10.6 miles per hour; Chicago: 10.3.

Q. What southern Miami County community served as a major testing and transmitting center for the nation's long distance telephone lines from 1894 till 1926?

A. Phoneton.

Q. Where was ethyl gasoline first marketed on February 2, 1923?

A. Dayton.

Q. What bug was named the official state insect in 1975?

A. The ladybug.

Q. What Ohio city contains the nation's largest soap factory?

A. Cincinnati.

Q. What heavily polluted Ohio river caught fire in 1969?

A. The Cuyahoga River (in Cleveland).

Q. The Hopewell Indian culture was named after what land-owner on whose farm the tribe's mounds were excavated?

A. Captain M. C. Hopewell.

Q. What natural gas well turned Findlay into a boomtown overnight in January of 1886?

A. The great Karg well.

Q. What two settlers brought fruit trees from Canada to establish orchards in the Berlin Heights area in 1812?

A. John Hoak and John Fleming.

Q. How many live births were recorded in Ohio in 1990?

A. 165,546.

Q. The Toledo Zoological Gardens are home to how many species of animals?

A. 560.

Q. What Ohio State University research facility is in Wooster?

A. Ohio Agricultural Research and Development Center.

Q. In the early 1800s, what did scientist William Goforth find in his excavations in the Cincinnati area?

A. Fossils of a giant sloth.

Q. Thomas White planted mulberry trees and built a cocoonery and factory to produce what kind of textile at Mount Pleasant in the early 1840s?

A. Silk.

Q. How many miles of rivers and streams are in Ohio?

A. Approximately 40,000.

Q. What educational institution pioneered combining molecules through chemical reactions?

A. University of Akron's Institute of Polymer Science.

Q. How many pounds of plug tobacco were produced in Middletown in 1903?

A. Seventeen million.

Q. The area around Mantua is Ohio's largest growing-region for what vegetable?

A. Potato.

Q. The Butterfly Festival held on Kelleys Island includes field research and tagging of what variety of migrating butterflies?

A. Monarch.

Q. What is Ohio's largest forestry exposition?

A. Paul Bunyan Show at Hocking Technical College, Nelsonville.

Q. What great accomplishment in television was announced at Toledo on July 10, 1949?

A. The first practical rectangular television tube.

———◆———

Q. In August of 1965, what variety of cryptocrystalline quartz was adopted as the official Ohio state gem?

A. Ohio flint.

———◆———

Q. To what record height did the flood waters of the Ohio River reach at Cincinnati in 1937?

A. 79.99 feet.

———◆———

Q. Residents of Reynoldsburg celebrate what agricultural event each September?

A. Birth of the commercially grown tomato.

———◆———

Q. How many natural gas wells are there in Ohio?

A. Over 11,000.

———◆———

Q. Of what material is the Ohio capitol building constructed?

A. Native limestone.

———◆———

Q. Akron was the home of Dr. Robert Holbrook Smith who helped co-found what organization?

A. Alcoholics Anonymous.

Q. What markings across the rocks of Kelleys Island attest to the Ice Age?

A. Glacial grooves.

Q. Exotic trees, shrubs, flowers, a cypress swamp, and a Japanese garden are part of what Newark attraction?

A. Dawes Arboretum.

Q. What Cleveland black inventor saved a number of lives with his "gas inhalator" device during a 1916 tunnel explosion?

A. Garrett A. Morgan.

Q. The original space suits worn by U.S. astronauts were made and fitted by what Akron company?

A. B. F. Goodrich.

Q. In 1836 Reese Thomas was the first to experiment with what type of clay from the Portsmouth area?

A. Fire clay for firebrick.

Q. On December 22, 1956, the Columbus Zoo became the site of the first birth in captivity of what type of primate?

A. A gorilla.

Q. What natural feature led to the naming of Salineville by early settlers?

A. Salt springs.

Q. What "weather forecasting" insects are honored each year with a festival at Vermilion?

A. Woollybear caterpillars.

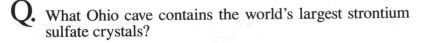

Q. What Ohio cave contains the world's largest strontium sulfate crystals?

A. Crystal Cave (Small Bass Island).

Q. What air and space museum is at Wapakoneta?

A. Neil Armstrong Museum.

Q. Completed in 1928 and stretching across the Ohio River at Kanauga, the "silver bridge" became the first in the nation protected by what kind of paint?

A. Aluminum.

Q. At Wilmington in the wettest southwestern part of the state, the average annual precipitation is how many inches?

A. Forty-four.

Q. The Wyandot Popcorn Museum is in what community?

A. Marion.

Q. Who established Ohio's first vineyards and strawberry patches in the Cincinnati area during the 1820s?

A. Nicholas Longworth, Sr.

Q. Harvey S. Firestone revolutionized farming techniques during the 1930s by developing and perfecting what new product?

A. Air-filled rubber tires for tractors and other farm implements.

Q. How many rose bushes are contained in Columbus' thirteen-acre Park of Roses?

A. 7,800.

Q. Dr. John Gilman at Marietta was the first to utilize what diagnostic aid for surgery?

A. X-rays.

Q. What city is the largest shipper of coal in the United States?

A. Toledo.

Q. Blue Hole, the flowing spring near Castalia, pours forth how many gallons daily?

A. Ten million.

Q. The nation's deepest limestone quarry is near what Ohio city?

A. Barberton.

Q. On September 20, 1985, what became the official Ohio state fossil?

A. The isotelus (commonly called trilobite).

Q. In what year was Cambridge-born astronaut John Glenn elected to the U.S. Senate from Ohio?

A. 1974.

Q. The Clifton Gorge State Nature Preserve is in what state park?

A. John Bryan State Park.

Q. Where in 1905 was the first successful blood transfusion performed by Dr. George Crile?

A. Cleveland.

Q. Where may Ohio's only moving sand dunes be seen?

A. Oak Openings Preserve, Swanton.

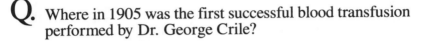

Q. How many hogs were processed in Cincinnati in 1845 and 1846?

A. 300,000 head.

Q. Where was Ohio's first commercial salt enterprise established in 1795?

A. On Salt Creek in Jackson County.

Q. How many soldiers died during the influenza epidemic that swept Camp Sherman near Chillicothe in 1918?

A. 1,177.

Q. Chewing gum was first patented by what Mount Vernon resident on December 28, 1869?

A. W. F. Semple.

Q. A small amount of what precious metal was discovered by Dr. James C. Lee near Bellville in 1853?

A. Gold.

Q. Other than appleseeds, Johnny Appleseed planted what kinds of seed to aid pioneer families?

A. Herbs (for medical remedies).

Q. What natural disaster destroyed all of the buildings in Jamestown in 1844?

A. Tornado.

Q. Who built a smelting furnace near the site of present-day Youngstown in 1804?

A. Daniel Heaton.

Q. What is the record high temperature in Ohio?

A. 113° F (at Thurman, July 4, 1897).

Q. What Oxford resident invented the revolutionary movable comb beehive?

A. Lorenzo Lorrain Langstroth.

Q. What famous inventor was born at Milan?

A. Thomas A. Edison.

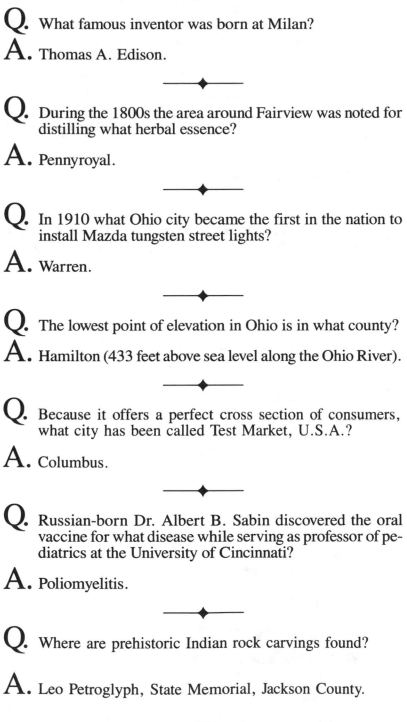

Q. During the 1800s the area around Fairview was noted for distilling what herbal essence?

A. Pennyroyal.

Q. In 1910 what Ohio city became the first in the nation to install Mazda tungsten street lights?

A. Warren.

Q. The lowest point of elevation in Ohio is in what county?

A. Hamilton (433 feet above sea level along the Ohio River).

Q. Because it offers a perfect cross section of consumers, what city has been called Test Market, U.S.A.?

A. Columbus.

Q. Russian-born Dr. Albert B. Sabin discovered the oral vaccine for what disease while serving as professor of pediatrics at the University of Cincinnati?

A. Poliomyelitis.

Q. Where are prehistoric Indian rock carvings found?

A. Leo Petroglyph, State Memorial, Jackson County.

Q. What process in the manufacture of shortening was first utilized at Cincinnati on August 15, 1911?

A. Hydrogenation.

Q. The only remaining B-70 aircraft is on display at what Dayton museum?

A. U.S. Air Force Museum.

Q. In what town did John Campbell build the first charcoal furnace north of the Ohio River to process iron ore in 1826?

A. Ironton.

Q. What is the approximate annual production of natural gas in Ohio?

A. Ninety-nine billion cubic feet.

Q. The Mosquito Creek Wildlife Area covers how many acres?

A. 8,000.

Q. In 1828 Dr. John M. Harris established the first of what kind of medical school in the world at Bainbridge?

A. A dental school.

Q. What is Ohio's most valuable mineral?

A. Coal.

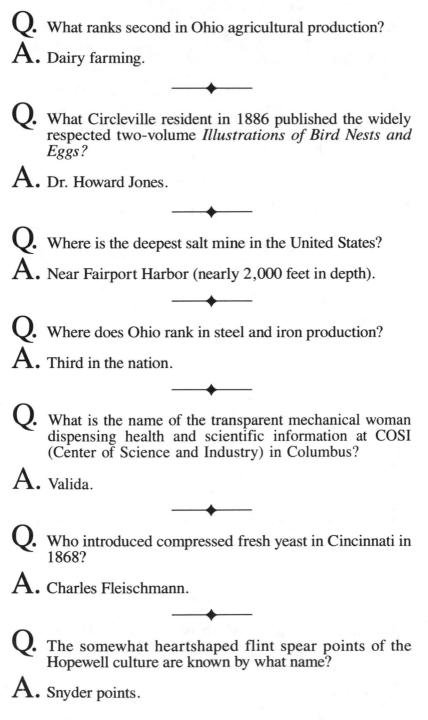

Q. What ranks second in Ohio agricultural production?

A. Dairy farming.

Q. What Circleville resident in 1886 published the widely respected two-volume *Illustrations of Bird Nests and Eggs?*

A. Dr. Howard Jones.

Q. Where is the deepest salt mine in the United States?

A. Near Fairport Harbor (nearly 2,000 feet in depth).

Q. Where does Ohio rank in steel and iron production?

A. Third in the nation.

Q. What is the name of the transparent mechanical woman dispensing health and scientific information at COSI (Center of Science and Industry) in Columbus?

A. Valida.

Q. Who introduced compressed fresh yeast in Cincinnati in 1868?

A. Charles Fleischmann.

Q. The somewhat heartshaped flint spear points of the Hopewell culture are known by what name?

A. Snyder points.

Q. Who drilled the first oil well in the Lima field in 1885?

A. Benjamin C. Faurot.

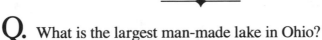

Q. Where does Ohio rank in the production of lime?

A. First in the nation.

Q. What is the largest man-made lake in Ohio?

A. Grand Lake (12,700 acres).

Q. Much of the sandstone used in New York's famous "brownstone fronts" of the 1880s and 1890s was quarried near what Holmes County community?

A. Glenmont.

Q. Where are the world's largest sulphur springs?

A. Green Springs.

Q. About what percent of Ohio's total land area is utilized by farming?

A. Seventy.

Q. The Columbus Zoo, which maintains some 31,500 specimens, is also the only zoo in the world housing how many generations of gorillas?

A. Four.

Q. What research facility of Ohio State University at Put-in-Bay studies the biology of the Great Lakes?

A. Franz Theodore Stone Laboratory.

Q. How many varieties of the buckeye tree are found in Ohio?

A. Three.

Q. What national forest covers large areas of southeastern Ohio?

A. Wayne National Forest.

Q. The Wright Brothers at Dayton were the first in history to construct what kind of aerodynamics research equipment?

A. A wind tunnel.

Q. Where was the first "automatic pilot" tested on October 8, 1929?

A. Cleveland.

Q. During the 1927 excavation of what Hopewell mound complex was a 28-pound ceremonial axe unearthed?

A. Seip Mound.

Q. What marsupial is found in Ohio?

A. The Virginia opossum.

Q. A model safehouse to teach fire safety and prevention is found at what Cincinnati institution?

A. Cincinnati Fire Museum.

Q. What two counties supply almost half of the coal mined in Ohio?

A. Belmont and Harrison counties.

Q. What is the total length of the Ohio River from its headwaters in Pennsylvania to its junction with the Mississippi River?

A. 967 miles.

Q. Approximately how many eggs are produced in Ohio each year?

A. Two billion.

Q. What Cleveland facility is operated under the National Aeronautics and Space Administration?

A. Lewis Research Center.

Q. At its peak during the late 1890s, what was the annual production from the Lima oil field?

A. Over twenty million barrels.

Q. What Galion inventor and manufacturer improved the telephone receiver and switchboard?

A. C. H. North.

Q. The unique Penguin Encounter is a part of what Cleveland area attraction?

A. Sea World marine park.

Q. How many gallons of brine from Salt Springs did early salt makers require to produce one pound of salt?

A. Ten to fifteen.

Q. What community is home to the Inniswood Botanical Garden and Nature Preserve?

A. Westerville.

Q. What technology museum filling four floors may be viewed in Columbus?

A. Center of Science and Industry.

Q. What variety of quail is found in the state?

A. Northern bobwhite.

Q. In 1893, what Geneva native made the first U.S. automobile sold abroad?

A. Ransom Eli Olds (a four-wheeled steam car sold in India).

Q. What is the name of the animal park in Jackson?

A. Noah's Ark Animal Park.

Ernie Couch and his wife, Jill, own and operate Consultx, a support firm for the publishing industry with specialties in advertising and graphic design. Together they compiled fourteen other trivia books.